KINGS OF THE HOME RUN

KINGS of the
HOME RUN

by Arthur Daley

G. P. PUTNAM'S SONS   New York

To my daughter, Kathy

CONTENTS

KINGS OF THE HOME RUN

1

The Home Run Is Born

ED BARROW was a big, tough, ham-fisted man who was strong of body and strong of mind when he managed the Boston Red Sox in 1918. That was the year when destiny first caught up with Barrow, a man who was to have a profound effect on baseball history because he later was to be the founder of the New York Yankee empire, a dynasty he brought to glory during the quarter of a century he served as its ruler.

In 1918, though, Barrow was operating on a smaller, more limited scale. And he had problems. The First World War was on, bringing manpower shortages to the big leagues. The Red Sox needed more batting power to go with their superior pitching.

Most brilliant of the Boston pitchers was a kid left-hander named Babe Ruth, a large and amiable youngster of twenty-four with a whistling fast ball, a wicked curve, remarkable control and no sense of responsibility. But this happy-go-lucky child of nature had been a 23-game winner in both 1916 and 1917 with successive earned run averages of 1.75 and 2.02, fantastically low.

No ordinary baseball man would dare contemplate experimenting with a gifted pitcher of such proven skills. But the bold and imaginative Barrow was smitten by an idea early in the 1918 season. He summoned Ruth to his room.

The Babe came fearfully. On all previous occasions Barrow had bawled him out unmercifully for infractions of training rules.

"What have I done now?" said the Babe, instantly on the defensive.

"Not a thing, Babe," said Barrow pleasantly. "I've just been toying with an idea. I won't force it on you, though. I'll leave the decision to you."

"Go ahead," said the Babe, completely relaxed.

"Our ball club needs hitting," said the manager, "and you're an exceptionally good hitter. You're big, strong and healthy. Why couldn't you play the outfield when you're not pitching?"

"You know how much I like to hit, Ed," said the young pitching phenomenon, eyes glistening at the prospect of swinging a bat every day. "Let's try it and see how it works."

That was a fateful day in the history of baseball. That was the day when the home run was born.

Sticklers for accuracy will disagree with that statement. They will insist that the home run has been an inherent part of the game from the very beginning. Technically they are as correct as the scientists who tell us that Thomas Alva Edison did not invent electricity. But Edison put it to practical use and gave mankind an entirely new way of life.

Babe Ruth did the same thing with the home run. He changed baseball's way of life. He opened up new vistas and widened the horizons. He triggered a revolution which was to alter an entire sport.

Not even the farseeing Barrow could have forecast the explosive effects his move would bring. Perhaps that was because the change came too gradually for quick recognition. It really took a couple of seasons for the impact to hit with shattering force.

Boston baseball writers viewed the switch of the Babe to the outfield with feelings akin to amusement. Some even offered to bet him that he'd be skulled by a fly ball before the season ended. He fooled them. He became a good out-fielder. Eventually he was to become a great one.

At that time the Bambino was a much trimmer athlete than he was later on. He stood six feet two but he weighed only 210 pounds. His shoulders were wide but his legs were slim and delicate. He was deceptively fast. Not only could he cover a tremendous amount of ground but he had a deadly throwing arm. In a short while no batter was trying to hit the ball in his direction or take extra bases on him.

In that season of 1918 the dead ball was in vogue. The Babe referred to it contemptuously as a "squash." It was not until Ruth demonstrated to the club owners the ir-resistible appeal of the home run as a gate attraction that the ball was given an injection of "jackrabbit juice." This new and lively ball was sneaked in during the 1920 and 1921 seasons, although the magnates piously denied such a change.

The Babe did not immediately open their eyes in that 1918 campaign as a part-time outfielder who played in a mere ninety-five games. However, he did contrive to tie Tillie Walker for the home run championship at eleven. This lowly figure brings into focus the total disregard and unimportance of the home run as a tactical weapon in the pre-Ruth era. By modern standards it must be considered quite shocking.

The greatest distance hitter of baseball's ancient days was Ed Delahanty of the Phillies. During the Gay Nineties he became something of a legend because he could hit a ball farther and oftener than most.

Although his lifetime statistical tables include practically all of his notable achievements, including his average of .408 in 1899, nowhere does it show how many homers he hit. They were not considered of sufficient consequence or interest to be tabulated. If you are curious as to how many the Great Delahanty slammed during his sixteen years in the majors, you need wonder no longer. He struck a mere ninety-eight.

Research on the home run output during baseball's ancient days is impossible. The first game of record is that between the Knickerbockers and the New York Club at the Elysian Fields in Hoboken, N. J., on June 19, 1846. The Knickerbockers were trounced, 23 to 1, in four innings. There was no box score. Yellowed history books merely list the names of the contestants plus the number of outs each made and the number of runs each scored. Not only are homers unmentioned but—this would horrify the modern ballplayer—no hits are mentioned, either.

Twenty-four years later, almost to the day, a baseball milestone was reached in Brooklyn. The first professional team, the famed Cincinnati Red Stockings, had gone through 130 games without defeat. Then they met the Atlantics on the Capitoline Grounds and lost in eleven innings, 8 to 7.

The crude box score of June 14, 1870, listed runs, hits, put-outs, assists and errors. But never a word on home runs. There just weren't enough of them to merit attention. In most historical accounts of the sport's earlier years it took an extraordinary feat to make the home run a newsworthy item.

Such was the case in 1894 when little Bobby Lowe of Boston became the first man to clout four in one game. Two years later big Ed Delahanty matched it. Not for thirty-six years was any slugger to do it again.

It was on Memorial Day of 1894 that Lowe achieved his date with immortality. The Boston Beaneaters, as they were then known, met the Cincinnati Red Stockings in the Hub, morning and afternoon games. Wee Bobby went hitless in the first game and took his wife to dinner at the North Boston Railroad Station. He gorged himself on a shore dinner, clams and lobster and fish. Then he returned to the ball park.

In the third inning he slammed one over the left-field fence. The side batted around and Lowe duplicated his feat in the same inning. In the fourth he did it again and in the sixth repeated the operation. The crowd went wild and showered the field with coins. The ballplayers stopped the game to pick up the loot, and the little second baseman was richer by $160.

"The fish dinner did it," said the superstitious Bobby to his teammates.

The next day he was back at the same table and again polished off an enormous shore dinner. He went hitless—and swore off fish for the rest of his life.

Delahanty's accomplishment was much more unusual. Among the reasons was the fact that he was in a tough ball park, the old Chicago field with a 35-foot wall that was topped by a 40-foot canvas designed to prevent the neighbors from peeking in at the ball game for free.

A powerful right-handed batsman, Big Ed was primarily a pull hitter whose target area was in left. But he hit the first pitch thrown him by Adonis Terry for a home run over the right-field fence. He singled to left in his next trip and then hammered a prodigious blast over the left-field scoreboard for his second homer.

"The longest ball ever hit in Chicago," wrote the Chicago press box experts.

With the score tied in the seventh the large Mr. Delahanty rifled a blast to left center. It scooted past Bill Lange, the fleet center fielder, and Big Ed thundered around the bases for an inside-the-park home run.

By this time the Chicago crowd was growing expectant and pulling for the visitor.

"Soak another, Del," they screamed as Delahanty stepped to bat in the ninth. "Soak another."

Del soaked one. It was a climbing line drive down the middle alley. It sailed onward and upward. It caromed off the roof of the clubhouse in center field and bounced over the fence.

This made for a unique collection. Four home runs—one to right, one to center, one to left and one inside the park.

The four-homer outbursts by Lowe and Delahanty were real stunners by the standards of yesteryear. This was the era of low-scoring games and strategic concepts were far different than they are now. Teams played for one run at a time. Often that one run was enough. Pitching was top-flight and pitchers went nine innings. The dead ball did not rocket off into space like a golf ball. Defenses were airtight and the "squash" that the Babe spoke about contributed to the defensive nature of the sport.

Batsmen were skilled artists then, not strong men. One of the best of the Gay Nineties was Wee Willie Keeler of the Baltimore Orioles, five feet four and 140 pounds.

"I hit 'em where they ain't," he said, a remark that has since become a baseball classic.

But that's the way they played ball in those days. The famed Orioles were the leaders, a group of hard-bitten performers who thought about the sport during every waking moment and then plotted and schemed. The chief thinker was John McGraw, the genius who later made the New York Giants the dominating team in the game.

Most of what is now known as "inside baseball" was invented by the Orioles, including the hit-and-run, the squeeze play and many less legal maneuvers, such as blocking, holding and tripping base runners.

This close-to-the-vest system was still in force when the American League was formed in 1901. Since the Americans stocked themselves with talent spirited away from the Nationals, both circuits played the same type of ball. The home run was relatively rare.

In the seventeen years prior to the switch of Babe Ruth to the outfield, all the hitters in the American League supplied a total of 2,653 home runs. In the one season of 1961 alone, the Americans produced a record total of 1,534 homers, and the combined total of the two leagues in that one campaign was an eye-catching 2,730.

Over the 162-game stretch Roger Maris popped sixty-one and Mickey Mantle clouted fifty-four. There also were six others who were over the forty mark. If the record books didn't prove differently, today's fan just couldn't believe what won distance hitting honors in yesteryear.

Tommy Leach of the Pittsburgh Pirates was the home run king of the National League in 1902. How many do you think he hit? You won't believe it but he was the swatsman supreme with only six homers.

Wahoo Sam Crawford of the Detroit Tigers could powder a ball farther than any man of his era.

"When I broke into the big leagues," Ty Cobb once told me, "Sam Crawford was the top dog in the meathouse."

That was in 1905. Three years later Crawford proved to Cobb and everyone else how deserving he was of the top dog distinction. He won the home run championship of his league. He hit seven homers.

Until the Babe made the home run his personal trademark, only two batters had passed twenty. Frank (Wildfire) Schulte of the Cubs had reached twenty-one in 1911 and Gavvy Cravath of the Phils had gone past it with twenty-four in 1915. Both were National Leaguers. The top American League figure was sixteen by Socks Seybold of the Athletics in 1902.

By 1919 Ruth's pitching assignments were rare; he was concentrating more and more on the outfield. This was to be his last season in a Red Sox uniform. He stunned the baseball world with twenty-nine homers. Not only had he achieved a record total but he was hammering the ball such fantastic distances that he left everyone gasping in disbelief.

The owner of the Red Sox was then Harry Frazee, a producer of theatrical turkeys. He was over his ears in debt and looked frantically around for help. He didn't have far to look.

At that time the New York Yankees were a dull, uninteresting club who shared the Polo Grounds with the darlings of New York, the exciting Giants of John McGraw. Although the Yanks kept losing their patronage battle with the Giants, they at least had fabulously wealthy owners in Col. Jacob Ruppert and Col. Tillinghast L'Hommedieu Huston, both millionaires. It was toward the colonels that the stony-broke Frazee turned. They whipped out their wallets and loaned Frazee $350,000 to pay off his more pressing debts and gave him $100,000 outright.

In exchange they received George Herman Ruth, a baseball player—and how! By the financial standards of that day, this was a staggering price. By modern standards, however, it's the same as getting all the gold at Fort Knox for a book of Green Stamps.

The Babe arrived in New York as the new king of the home run. Twenty-nine homers! Wowie! The fans were in a fever of anticipation. No one could break that record—unless it were the Babe himself. So the customers flocked to the Polo Grounds to watch and their enthusiasm was so contagious that the big guy caught it.

As early as July 19 the Babe tagged Dickie Kerr of the White Sox for homer No. 30. He had broken his own record with little more than half a season played. Every homer that followed was merely icing on the cake. And the Babe piled on plenty of icing. On September 29 he connected off Dave Keefe of the Athletics for his last round-trip shot of the campaign. It was No. 54.

The Colossus of Clout, the Sultan of Swat, the Maharajah of Maul—it mattered not what title they gave him. The Babe was supreme, off in a class by himself. The club owners vigorously denied that they had hopped up the old dead ball and replaced it with the jackrabbit or lively ball of today. To a certain extent the statistics would seem to support them.

Ruth hit fifty-four homers. Next best was George Sisler of the St. Louis Browns with merely nineteen. And only fourteen other men in both major leagues were in double figures, with ten homers or more.

Even more impressive than that, perhaps, is the comparison of the Babe's individual home run production with that of entire teams. He outslugged fourteen of the fifteen other ball clubs in the majors. Only the Phillies with sixty-four homers escaped his sweep and they were operating out of midget Baker Bowl which wasn't much bigger than a telephone booth.

The club owners also realized for the first time that there was more than just glamour in the Ruthian smashes. There were solid profits in them, too. Although the Polo Grounds then had a capacity of only 33,000, the Yankees drew the unheard-of attendance of 1,289,422. And Ruth also packed all the ball parks on the road.

In the following season the Bambino did what everyone said was impossible. He broke his record of fifty-four with fifty-nine. He still outdistanced all pursuit but the force of example was having an effect. For the first time five hitters went over the 20 mark—Ken Williams and Bob Meusel with twenty-four, George Kelly and Curt Walker with twenty-three and Rogers Hornsby with twenty-one.

The home run tempo was stepping up in both leagues. In 1921 it more than doubled what it had been two years earlier, reaching 460 for the Nationals and 477 for the Americans. Then it soared up another notch in 1922 at 530 and 524. But George Herman Ruth was not the grandiose contributor that season he should have been.

The acclaim he received after his fifty-nine homers was so giddy that it turned his head. Impressed by his own importance, he defied Judge Kenesaw Mountain Landis, the Commissioner, and went on a barnstorming tour after the World Series despite orders to the contrary. For this disobedience he was suspended by the Judge for the first thirty days of the 1922 season.

The handicap was too much to overcome. Not only did the Babe start late but he started badly. His batting average shrank from .378 to .315 and his homer output from fifty-nine to thirty-five. That last item wasn't sufficient to win the home run championship. Ken Williams of the Browns took it with thirty-nine.

By this time, however, the Yankees were cutting deep inroads into the Giant popularity, and McGraw grew jealous of the Babe's magic.

"Get them out of here," he snapped to Charlie Stoneham, the Giant owner. McGraw not only bossed his players but his club owner as well. So Stoneham issued an eviction notice to his tenants.

Thus was the Yankee Stadium forced into being. "The House that Ruth Built," they called it. Naturally enough, the Babe presided at the christening ceremonies, slamming a game-winning homer on opening day of 1923.

But he set different goals that season. Instead of leading the league in distance clouting, he'd go for hits. He got plenty of them and attained the highest batting average of his career, a gaudy .393. Unfortunately it was not quite enough to win the batting championship. Harry Heilmann took that with an even gaudier .403. But the Babe did regain his home run title from Ken Williams with forty-one, a total that had to seem modest in comparison to his fifty-nine of a couple of seasons earlier.

A year later it was forty-six homers and a .376 average, which was sufficient to win the batting crown. However, there was no extraordinary rise in the home run totals of the major leagues, but the explosion was soon to come, almost as if a slow-burning fuse were inching its way to set off the big blast. None saw it coming and that's why it was such a shock.

The year was 1927. The Babe was a portly veteran of thirty-three who had not made a serious challenge to his home run record of fifty-nine during the intervening seasons. Most experts thought he had passed his peak.

But in 1927 the Yankees bobbed up with what was undoubtedly the greatest team ever assembled. A broad-shouldered young man had joined the Yanks a few years earlier and he was just coming into his own that season, a fellow who terrorized the pitchers just as the Babe did. His name was Lou Gehrig. This pair supplied the most awesome one-two punch in baseball history.

He provided a challenge that the Babe could not resist because Gehrig, the Iron Horse, was baseball's leading home run hitter for a good part of the season. But all the Yankees were on the upswing. They crushed the Philadelphia Athletics, their chief rivals, in the opening game and then dominated proceedings until the final day. They hammered out a record 110 victories and won the pennant by the unbe-

lievable margin of 19 games. They also had a rather unbelievable team batting average of .307.

They didn't do it with the wrist-snapping finesse of the
old-timers. They did it with brute strength as they boomed
out homers, triples and doubles.

"No one on the ball club will talk to me," said Jumping
Joe Dugan, the witty third baseman. "I'm in disgrace. I only
hit singles."

He was joking, of course. But Yankee slugging was so
overwhelming a trait that the press box pundits hung a
nickname on them, "Murderers' Row." This could be the
most important nickname ever coined, because it captured
everyone's imagination and blinded the fans so that they
saw nothing except the big wallop.

Yet here was a team that had magnificent pitching and
as slick a defense as may ever have been assembled. Earle
Combs was a gazelle in center field and only a weak arm
prevented him from ranking as one of the finest outfielders
ever to perform. But he didn't need it. The far-ranging Bob
Meusel in left had one of the great arms in baseball history.
In right was the Babe, a superb ball hawk and deadly accurate thrower. Dugan was an acrobat at third; Mark Koenig and Tony Lazzeri an incomparable double-play combination; Lou Gehrig a hard-working indomitable first
baseman.

But the Yankee trademark was the long hit that Murderers' Row kept manufacturing, and baseball never was
the same again. The Yanks scorned the tight-to-the-vest
system of John McGraw and the old Orioles. They didn't
play for one run at a time; they went for them in bunches.

Combs had more hits than anyone else in the league, 231;
Gehrig batted in the most runs, 175; Gehrig had the most
doubles, 52; Combs had the most triples, 23, and the incomparable Babe broke his own home run record with 60.

"I'd never have set that record if it hadn't been for the Dutchman," said the Babe many years later. "He was really getting beef behind the ball and finished with forty-seven home runs. At a time we were neck and neck so that pitchers couldn't walk me any more because Lou was next in the batting order. I really put wood to the ball in September and left him behind."

He sure did. In the September homestretch, when the pressure was most intense, the Sultan of Swat came through with a matchless haul of seventeen homers. The last of these was No. 60, the day before the season ended. It came off Tom Zachary, a wily left-hander on Washington.

In his first at bat the Babe walked. Then he drove out two singles and was running out of time because Zachary had resolved not to give him one good pitch all afternoon. He didn't, either.

"The ball Babe hit for his sixtieth homer," said Zachary afterward, "was the kind of ball no other batter would have tried for. It was a curve ball, high and straight at him. You might call it a beanball. Instead of stepping back he waded right into the ball. He lunged at it before it ever got to the plate and pulled it around into the stands. I don't see yet how he did it. He never hit a worse ball in his life, nor one that would be more difficult to hit into the stands."

There are statistics relating to Ruth's 60-homer season that must be introduced because they demonstrate that the craze for homers had not enveloped the big leagues with any degree of completeness.

Ruth's sixty was more than the total output of twelve of the fifteen other clubs. Ranking third behind him and Gehrig in the American League was Tony Lazzeri with eighteen. The Nationals did a little better as Hack Wilson of the Cubs and Cy Williams of the Phils had thirty and Rogers Hornsby had twenty-six.

The home run king always gets a royal welcome at home plate. Here Duke Snider prepares to receive the plaudits of his Dodger retinue.

But the impact of the Ruthian feat had rocked the baseball world. Furthermore Gehrig's forty-seven demonstrated that mortal men—the Babe was considered a demigod—could also reach up into the home run stratosphere.

Within three seasons both leagues had set records for total homers, 754 by the Nationals and 673 by the Americans. Before the outbreak of World War II the pattern was unmistakable. The distance sluggers were beginning to take over. The National League had a top mark of 892 and the Americans of 883, although the Americans were consistently higher during the thirties.

After the war the talent scouts began to give special emphasis to a certain extra in prospects they inspected. Like scouts of earlier generations, they judged a boy on his ability to run and his ability to throw, these being God-given attributes which cannot be taught. More than ever before, though, they looked for the ability to *hit with power*. No longer was mere hitting enough by itself. Distance was a new consideration.

Furthermore, the National League, which had grown decidedly inferior, had been reorganized by its then president, Ford Frick. Wealthy owners moved in and the pendulum began to swing in the other direction. The older league began to grab for the musclemen and dominated home run statistics until an expanded American League finally whisked past in 1961.

Before World War II only four men crashed more than fifty homers in a season. They were the Babe with sixty, fifty-nine and fifty-four; Jimmy Foxx with fifty-eight and fifty; Hank Greenberg with fifty-eight and Hack Wilson with fifty-six.

After it the step-up in production was notable, climaxed as it was with Roger Maris' sixty-one over the longer schedule in 1961. The chronological listing shows Johnny Mize with fifty-one in 1947, Ralph Kiner with fifty-one in 1947 and fifty-four in 1949, Willie Mays with fifty-one in 1955, Mickey Mantle with fifty-two in 1956 and fifty-four in 1961.

What sharpens the contrast between the pre-Ruth and post-Ruth eras are the team totals. Before the Babe triggered his revolution, no ball club had ever combined more than seventy-three home runs in a season. By 1947 the New York Giants had raised the record to 221 under the managerial regime of Master Melvin Ott, himself a home run hitter.

Nine years after the Giant record was set, a new batch

of explosive sluggers erupted in Cincinnati, guided by that youthful managerial genius, Birdie Tebbetts. He kept them in the pennant fight until the final week, but as soon as the championship was out of reach he switched objectives. He took dead aim at the Giant homer record.

On the next-to-the-last day of the campaign, the Redleg total had reached 220 and the Cincy Clout Circus was making a runaway of a game with the Cubs. In the ordinary course of events a manager will never use a pinch hitter when winning by a lopsided score. But this situation was out of the ordinary.

Birdie barked out an order and sent Smoky Burgess, the muscular catcher, into the fray as a pinch hitter for one of his lightweight hitters.

"You know why I'm having you hit?" said Birdie.

"Certainly," said the unconcerned Smoky. "You want me to hit a home run so that we'll tie the record."

"Right," said Birdie. "Homer or nothing."

So Smoky hit a home run.

When the Yankees also reached homer No. 221 during the 1961 season, they were so distracted by the Maris-Mantle private assault on the Babe's mark that it practically sneaked up on them unawares. Yogi Berra hit it, crossed the plate and jogged to the dugout.

"I hope you realize, little man," said the lighthearted Whitey Ford, "that you just hit No. 221 for us. It will make you famous as the guy whose homer tied the record."

"Holy gee," said the flabbergasted Yogi. "Did I?"

The tie breaker was produced by Moose Skowron but everyone was aware of its significance by then. The grinning Moose reached the bench.

"You shouldn't have done that, Moose," said Bobby Richardson.

"Why not?" said the Moose, not expecting a ribbing from the quiet Richardson but instinctively suspicious.

"Because I wanted to do it myself," said Wee Bobby with a straight face. Richardson had hit only six homers in his entire big league career. Everyone laughed.

The Yanks kept booming away. By the time they'd reached the 154-game deadline, they had raised the onetime joint record of Giants and Reds from 221 to 231. They finished the longer campaign with a total of 240.

It was not only the big leagues which were affected by the Ruth example. It penetrated all the way down to the sandlots. If there had been any Little Leaguers in those days, it would have affected them, too.

Before the turn of the century the ideal of the kids of America was Wee Willie Keeler and the other masters of the hit-'em-where-they-ain't school. A few decades later it was Ty Cobb, another artist at placing the ball beyond the reach of the fielders.

The kids copied their styles and became what is known as "choke" hitters. They would choke up their grip on the bat, grasping the handle a couple of inches above the knob. Bats were thicker-handled and heavier, most weighing more than 40 ounces. The Babe, bigger and stronger than most, sometimes went as high as 48 ounces. Cobb preferred 42.

But the Babe didn't choke his grip. He held the bat at the very end in order to get leverage. He swung from his heels, uncoiling with the lash of a high-tension spring. Soon every small boy in every vacant lot was trying to imitate the Sultan of Swat. Among them were the future big-leaguers. To them the home run was everything.

The Babe used a thin-handled bat with a heavy barrel. Everyone wanted a thin-handled bat although the weight was reduced. The fashionable bat came closer to 36 ounces.

Then came a discovery not too many years ago. Although the lively ball had been in use for a quarter of a century, it took Ernie Banks of the Chicago Cubs to sponsor the lively bat. At least he's the one who has been given credit for it.

Banks is a tall, slim 170-pounder with hair-trigger reflexes and remarkable wrist action. In his first full season of 1954 he hit nineteen homers. A year later he boomed all the way up to forty-four homers.

There are no secrets in baseball; the big-leaguers are much too curious. That's how they learned that Banks was using a 30-ounce bat. It had all the whip and propulsive force of a golf club. This started a stampede toward lighter bats and few major-leaguers of today use a bat as high as 34 ounces. The average is probably 32.

If the Ruthian revolution increased the output of homers tenfold, it ruined hitting for average. Not only did the Babe slam far more homers than any man in history, 714, but he also struck out more often than any man in history, 1,330. That he was able to produce a high lifetime average of .342 is due entirely to the fact that he was a freak of nature who could defy the rules and get away with it. Ordinary men can't. Most have to choose between hitting for distance or hitting for average. No better example exists than Roger Maris, who spurned the average and went for distance.

This is reflected in the fact that there have rarely been more than a half dozen .300 hitters in each league over the past decade while batting championships have been won with marks as low as .320 and .325.

But back in 1930, before the home run craze had taken a stranglehold on the majors, the situation was radically different. The Americans furnished thirty-three players who batted over .300, topped by Al Simmons of the Athletics with .381. The Nationals had forty-three men over .300

and the high man was Bill Terry of the Giants with .401. Poor Babe Herman batted .393 for the Dodgers that year and was hardly noticed.

Ruth's responsibility for the rise in home run production also is mirrored in a less apparent, more left-handed fashion. He attracted bigger crowds than baseball ever had known before. Attendance zoomed everywhere. Seating capacities had to be increased. Yet enlarging the stands was possible in only one direction.

Since most ball parks are surrounded by streets and avenues, it was impossible to push back into public thoroughfares. So the push was inward—toward the playing fields. Every such encroachment brought home plate closer to the stands and reduced the home run range.

Some magnates also shrank the playing surfaces not of necessity but merely to encourage homers. After Hank Greenberg, a fading home run hitter, joined the Pittsburgh Pirates, the owners tailored Forbes Field to help him with an area which became known as "Greenberg Gardens."

This was a fence-inside-a-fence and shortened Hank's left-field target by thirty feet. Frank Lane built an inner chicken-wire barrier in Chicago's Comiskey Park to invite home runs. But when enemy hitters accepted his bid with far more enthusiasm and frequency than his White Sox, Frantic Frankie withdrew the invitation. He tore down his fence.

Griffith Stadium in Washington was an oversize playpen of formidable proportions. But as soon as Calvin Griffith assembled long-ball hitters on his Senators, he moved in the fences as much as thirty-eight feet in order to help them.

In the expansion of the American League, however, Griff switched his franchise to the Twin Cities of Minneapolis and St. Paul, leaving Griffith Stadium to a newly formed team. The new Senators consisted mainly of singles hitters. So the fences went back to where they originally had been located, on the sound theory that only visiting clubs would profit by too neighborly fences.

For the most part, though, the trend always has been toward contraction. One typical example is Cleveland. When the Indians moved permanently into the huge Municipal Stadium, the power alleys from left center to right center presented far too distant targets, the footage to the stands being 435, 450 and 435. Bill Veeck promptly installed a storm fence from foul line to foul line, cutting down the playing surface so drastically that the power alleys were reduced to 380, 410 and 380. This put homers on a bargain-basement scale at reduced prices of between 40 and 55 feet.

Babe Ruth triggered the revolution that changed the face of baseball. The introduction of the lively ball came quickly but other changes to aid in home run production came at slower pace—the shrinkage of the fields, the lighter bat and the like. His most profound contribution, perhaps, was his psychological impact. He altered the thinking processes of every baseball-playing man and boy in the United States.

He became the greatest national sports hero America has ever known. At a time when the average major league ballplayer earned no more than $5,000 a year, the Babe earned $80,000—and was worth every penny. He pulled the entire salary scale up with him and demonstrated the rewards that accompany the home run.

So shattering was the effect the Babe had on the sport that no player who preceded him is to be found on the list of leading home run hitters. That is true whether analysis is made of the select group of 300-plus homers or the larger 200-plus group. Not one old-timer had the muscle to crowd his way in. This means that no pre-Ruth slugger rates among the top hundred homer hitters of all time.

Ruth showed the way with his 714 homers and the others followed—but not too closely. Jimmy Foxx with 534, Ted Williams with 521 and Mel Ott with 511 are the only others over the 500 mark. Lou Gehrig at 493 and Stan Musial at 444 are the lone members of the 400 grouping. In the 300-plus category come Duke Snider, Mickey Mantle, Eddie Mathews, Ralph Kiner, Joe DiMaggio, Gil Hodges, Johnny Mize, Yogi Berra, Hank Greenberg, Willie Mays, Al Simmons, Rogers Hornsby and Chuck Klein. That's the full membership.

It's time now to take a more intimate look at the Kings of the Home Run in order to see what made them tick as hitters and as human beings. They are a fascinating group who have contributed richly to baseball history with drama, humor, color, achievement, and the sheer force of personality.

There can be only one logical starting point, the richest contributor of all—George Herman Ruth, the immortal, unforgettable and implausible Babe.

2

KING GEORGE

George Herman (Babe) Ruth

IF Babe Ruth was born with two strikes on him, destiny just didn't have the heart to slip a third strike over the plate. Because he could bash a ball farther than any man who ever lived, he swung his way clear from slum surroundings to fame and fortune.

It was a discouraging start, though. The Babe's father was a saloonkeeper in Baltimore and the Babe spent the first seven years of his life living over the saloon—or in it. His parents were so busy serving drinks to longshoremen, roughnecks and waterfront bums that they had no time for their son. Whatever he learned, he learned from the wrong people. He chewed tobacco at the age of seven.

Although he said, "I hardly knew my parents," they soon knew they couldn't handle him. He was listed as an incorrigible and sent—at the tender age of seven—to St. Mary's Industrial School in Baltimore, a haven for what would be known today as juvenile delinquents. This was to change the course of his life and prove to be his salvation.

"It was at St. Mary's," he wrote, "that I met and learned to love the greatest man I have ever known. His name was Matthias—Brother Matthias of the Xaverian Order, a Catholic order which concentrates on work among underprivileged boys here and in Europe."

Brother Matthias was all man and there was a lot of him, too. He was six feet six and weighed 250 pounds. Heavenly

voices must have whispered to him to take an interest in the
saloonkeeper's son, and the Babe became his pet. He studied
what few gifts the boy had and recognized an uncanny talent
for playing baseball. So the huge brother hit fungoes to
him or pitched to him and brought him along so fast that the
Babe was on the twelve-year-old team when he was only
eight and on the sixteen-year-old team when he was twelve.
And, of all things, he was a catcher, a left-handed catcher
at that. Oh, yes. He also pitched.

One day in 1914, Joe Engel of the Washington Senators
was invited back to Mount St. Mary's College to pitch for
the alumni against the varsity. There was a preliminary
game that day, involving the team from the nearby Industrial School, and Engel's eyes popped.

A tall, gangling kid with coal-black hair pitched for the
orphanage—it was known more as an orphanage than a
reform school—and fanned eighteen or twenty batters.
Then, still in baseball uniform, he joined the orphanage
band and proceeded to belabor a huge bass drum with more
enthusiasm than rhythm.

On the train back to Washington that night Engel encountered Jack Dunn, manager of the Baltimore Orioles,
then a top minor league team. Dunn promptly asked the
time-honored question.

"See anyone who looked good?" he said.

"Yeah," said Engel. "That orphan asylum team had a
big kid pitching for them and he's got real stuff. He also
can beat the stuffings out of a bass drum."

"You don't remember his name, do you?" asked Dunn.

"I think they called him Ruth," said Engel.

There was irony to that. Engel was to become one of the
most famous of all baseball scouts. Yet here he was, touting
the hottest prospect he ever would see—for free. Shortly
thereafter he ran into Dunn again.

"Did you sign that kid yet?" said Engel.

"Who?" said Dunn, not quite understanding the question.

"That kid I saw at the Mount," said Engel heatedly. "The left-handed kid who pitched and beat the stuffings out of the drum afterwards."

"Oh, him," said Dunn. "Yeah, I signed him. And let me tell you, Joe. He's a very mediocre drummer."

The Babe was fearful of failure when he got the bid to join the Orioles. But Brother Matthias was not.

"You'll make it, George," he said in fond farewell.

The first contract he signed was for $600. Dunn made the offer and the Babe was flabbergasted.

"Y-y-y-you mean you're gonna pay me to play baseball?" he stammered. He'd have played for nothing. He never really changed, even when he was holding out for $80,000 a year. He still would have played for nothing.

The Babe was a wild one who overdid everything. His appetites were huge. He could wolf down a dozen hot dogs and a dozen Cokes at once. He wasn't a drinker but when he drank, he drank too much and partying lasted all night. He was a freak of nature. Those who tried to imitate his high living paid the penalty of losing their big league skills in a couple of seasons. The Babe lasted for twenty-two years.

The man was fantastic. As a kid pitcher for Baltimore he once spent the night on the town and never went to bed. Sleepless and woozy, he reported to the ball park and took a cold shower to straighten out. Then he pitched a gaudy two-hitter and won the game, 1 to 0, with a home run in the ninth. Not even the fictional Frank Merriwell would have done anything so preposterous.

Miller Huggins, a mild-mannered little man, was the manager of the Yankees when Ruth joined the ball club. Although the Babe had had high respect for Ed Barrow, his manager in Boston, he had none for Hug and held him in contempt.

Eventually Ruth's violation of training rules ruined the morale of the ball club. Huggins dreaded the thought of a showdown, but he knew it had to come.

Then one day Huggins confided to the baseball writers that he'd caught Ruth cold when he returned at breakfast from a nightlong party. He would fine him after the game. He never did, though.

"How can you fine a guy like that?" asked Hug in despair.

The Babe had hit three of the longest home runs of his career.

But the showdown was on its way. One afternoon, player and manager exchanged heated words.

"If you were any bigger," shouted the Babe to the little Miller, "I'd punch you in the nose."

"If I were any bigger," said Huggins, standing up to the hulking brute in front of him, "you wouldn't dare try."

Huggins fined him $5,000 for insubordination. The angry Babe rushed back to New York. He would see Colonel Jacob Ruppert, the owner, and Ed Barrow, the general manager. They would put Huggins in his place by canceling the fine. But they gave Babe the cold shoulder and pledged full support to Huggins. The Babe slunk out, quiet and subdued.

This was the making of Hug as a manager. Ruth began to give his skipper the respect he deserved and soon developed an affection for the little fellow. That was much more in accord with the Big Guy's nature because he was a friendly, generous, warmhearted man who liked everyone. Most of all, he liked the kids.

One year the Yankees stopped off in Vicksburg, Mississippi, on their way home from spring training. A courtly old Southerner, who looked as though he might have stepped forth from the pages of *Gone With the Wind,* approached the Babe.

"My grandson, suh," he drawled, "is ailin'." Then he went on to tell how the little boy was nigh to death and nothing would give to him the will to live but an autographed baseball from the Sultan of Swat, the hero the youngster had adored.

"Sure, doc," boomed the Babe in his deep bass voice. "Be glad to. I'll give him a couple of autographed balls. Better still, I'll take 'em to him. Gotta car, doc? Let's go."

They went twelve miles in a driving rainstorm to cheer up a dying boy whose very existence Ruth was unaware of a few moments before. The Babe's magic worked, too. The boy lived.

Ruth was constantly doing things like that but he never would allow such charitable visits to be publicized. One day Arthur Mann, the baseball writer, overheard him promise on the phone to drop in on the children's ward of a hospital. The Babe spotted Mann as he hung up the phone and grabbed the writer by the shirtfront.

"If you print a word about this," he roared, "I'll kill you." No words were printed. Even in the good things he did the Babe was grandiose.

The Bambino once told me how he earned $40,000 for a thirteen-week vaudeville tour. Of that sum he spent $50,000 in expenses. If that's bad arithmetic, at least it's good Babe Ruth.

In his early years the King of Klout spent his money as fast—or faster—than he earned it. But once Christy Walsh took charge of the Ruthian purse as his business manager, extravagance stopped. An annuity was started. Although the Babe was not a wealthy man when he died, he was able to live in luxurious comfort. His biggest salary haul came in 1930 when he held out for an $80,000 contract.

Colonel Ruppert, a tough bargainer, refused to give it to him. After a while the Babe's sportswriting friends began to worry. The stock market had crashed the year before and the country had plunged into the depression. They warned their pal that his demands were in bad taste and would backfire on him from a publicity standpoint.

"That's more money than Hoover gets as President of the United States," said one writer, trying to prove his point.

"What's Hoover got to do with it?" growled the Babe. He thought for a moment and brightened. Then he added, "Besides, I had a better year than he did anyway."

He sure did. So he got the eighty thousand.

The writers couldn't resist the Babe anyway. He was so colorful and did things in such dramatic fashion that he made their work so much easier and their words so much more avidly read. Every baseball fan in the country—as well as many non-baseball fans—wanted to read about this unbelievable character.

Most unbelievable incident of all, perhaps, came in the 1932 World Series with the Chicago Cubs. The Yankees won their pennant with relative ease while the Cubs had to struggle. The move that saved the Bruins was the acquisition of Mark Koenig, onetime Yankee shortstop. But when the players voted on cutting up their World Series shares, they cut him in for only half a share. Since the Yankees always have been generous in slicing the World Series loot, they did not take kindly to the treatment their old buddy received. When the Cubs came on the field to warm up before the first game, the Yanks let fire a verbal barrage. Loudest of all was the Babe when he spotted Koenig.

"Hiya, Mark," bellowed the Babe in a booming voice

that almost shook the steel girders. "Who are those cheap-skates with you? What a bunch of nickel nursers! Lousy bunch of misers!"

Ruth curled the ears of the Cubs with his taunts. The other Yankees took up the cry and the language became pretty rough. The Chicagoans poured out the insults in self-defense until everyone was screaming like fishwives.

The Cubs, shaken by the Ruthian charges, lost the first two games. The Series moved to Chicago and Cub fans, reading about the bristling feud, were in a lather. At game time the Bronx Bombers were showered with imprecations —and overripe vegetables. The worst razzing came to Ruth, who was madder than ever because fans had spat on his wife.

In the fourth inning he came to bat with Earl Combs on base and with Charlie Root pitching against him. The jeering became louder and the Babe stepped out of the box and pointed toward the bleachers. Root blazed one in. The Babe called the strike even before the umpire did. The mob howled louder. Root did it again. Once more Ruth signaled the strike. Then he pointed to the bleachers once more— and hit the next pitch exactly where he pointed, high into the center-field bleachers for a home run.

"It was the funniest and proudest moment of my life," the Babe said afterward. "When I looked over into the Cub dugout, they'd fallen back as though I'd machine-gunned them."

One post-game interviewer was still shaking in the club-house afterward.

"Gosh, Babe," he said. "What a thing to do, calling a shot like that and making it. Suppose you had missed?"

"Good Lord," said the Babe. "I never thought of that."

To him the impossible was always within reach.

Once during his early years with the Yankees, the Babe

crashed a shot down the foul line at the Polo Grounds. It caromed off a girder down which the foul line was painted. The Babe began to trot around the bases.

"Foul ball!" shouted Billy Evans, the plate umpire.

"What was wrong with that, Billy?" yelled the Babe in protest.

"It was an inch to the foul side of the line," said Billy, the best American League umpire of his era.

"Okay," said the Babe, returning to the batter's box. "Watch this one closely. It will be an inch fair."

The Bambino hit a carbon copy of the first one. He looked back at the umpire.

"Go ahead," said Billy. "It was an inch fair."

An accident? Of course, it was. But the accuracy of the forecast demonstrates how extraordinary the Ruth legend has become. He did nothing to hinder its growth.

The Yankees were locked in a 1–1 tie with the White Sox in Chicago and the game dragged on for inning after inning until it reached the thirteenth. Mark Roth, the traveling secretary, was beginning to sweat blood. Train time was at hand and the stationmaster could delay the train no longer.

The Babe emerged from the dugout to take his turn at bat and he noticed Roth squirming in a box alongside.

"Whatsa matter, Mark?" he boomed. "You sick or something?"

"Yes," moaned Mark. "If you bums don't finish this game soon, we'll miss the train."

"Why didn't you say so sooner?" roared the Babe. "I'll get us outta here."

So the Big Guy led off the fourteenth inning with a home run. The Yankees caught the train.

Ford Frick is the Commissioner of Baseball, a man dedicated to preserving the sanctity of the sport and to keeping it clear of any taint, real or imaginary. But Frick's father went to his grave at the age of ninety-five with the conviction that there was something untrustworthy about baseball. Who gave him such an outlandish notion? Babe Ruth, of course.

The Yankees were playing an exhibition game in Fort Wayne and Frick, then a baseball writer, decided he'd take his aging parent to the ball game. Late in the fray the Babe wandered over to where the elder Frick was sitting.

"Getting tired, Pop?" he said. "Tell you what I'll do for you. See those railroad tracks over there?"

He pointed to where a freight train was chugging along beyond the center-field fence some 400 feet away.

"Pop," announced the Babe, "I'm gonna hit one onto those tracks."

He did, of course. But he forever destroyed the faith of the old gentleman, who reasoned that there had to be something fundamentally wrong with a sport which permitted its players to call the turn with such uncanny accuracy.

Power? The Babe had it to burn. Hod Lisenbee threw him a pitch and the Babe hit it with projectile force. It shot back through the box with such velocity that it went screaming *between* the pitcher's legs and sailed serenely *over* the head of the center fielder. You don't believe it possible, eh? Okay. Wait a minute.

Although it's virtually a violation of union rules for a writer to deflate his own story, that Lisenbee episode does require both explanation and expansion. When I first wrote about that incident, incredulous letter writers bombarded me with demands for date, place and proof. That was what I had the least of—to be blunt about it. Yet I knew it was more than just another Ruthian legend.

And who should come galloping to the rescue but Hod Lisenbee himself. He wrote me from Atlanta, Georgia, that the tale was true, but . . .

Just before he delivered the pitch for the Cleveland Indians, Tris Speaker tried one of his pet tricks. The Gray Eagle was probably the greatest center fielder of all. He was so swift on swooping back on fly balls that he played a shallower center than most. This also helped him sneak in on second base and trap any unwary base runner who had taken too big a lead. Just as Speaker closed in toward the base, Lisenbee fired his pitch to the plate. It was over the graying noggin of the Gray Eagle that the ball soared for an inside-the-park home run.

No matter how it happened, though, it still is a stupendous feat, impossible for anyone but the Babe.

Everything about the man was majestic, including his strikeouts. Whether he fanned or homered, he did it in Ruthian fashion. He was the only man in baseball history who could make a crowd gurgle and gasp by striking out.

When he popped up, his pop-ups gained greater altitude than anyone else's. Before Jimmie Dykes settled down at third to become one of the true artists at the position, he broke in with the Philadelphia Athletics as a second baseman. He was patrolling that post one afternoon when the Babe popped up.

Dykes spotted the ball as it brushed against a low-hanging cloud. He circled underneath, waiting for it to come down. He waited and waited and waited; his circling became more frantic. Then he lunged frantically and fell down.

The Babe chugged into second base with the shortest—but highest double—on record, laughing as he ran.

"Nice work, James," said mild-mannered Connie Mack to Dykes afterward. "If that ball had ever landed on your skull, it would have killed you."

Eddie Rommel, master of the knuckleball, practically had the Babe breaking his back in missing his first two pitches. So Ruth shortened his grip and just punched at the ball with a half swing. It went into the stands for a home run.

Only one pitcher ever hog-tied him completely, Hub Pruett of the St. Louis Browns. With a tricky screwball the left-hander was in complete control. He faced Ruth eighteen times and fanned him sixteen times. Only once did he ever throw him a curve. The Babe hit it out of the park.

When Fred Haney was a rookie with the Browns, he sliced a feeble little fly ball to right. The wind lifted it into the stands and it barely cleared the barrier for a home run. Haney was overjoyed. As Ruth trotted past him at the inning's end, frisky Fred gave him the needle.

"Howja like that, you big stiff?" shouted Haney. "Now you're only forty-four home runs ahead of me."

Ruth said not a word. Haney kept taunting him and Ruth kept ignoring him as the Babe moved up to the plate. Immediately he boomed one into the upper deck, a soaring blast of Ruthian proportions. The Babe jogged around the bases. As he passed Haney at third, he spoke for the first time.

"How do we stand now, kid?" he asked.

When Walter Johnson was pitching for the Washington Senators, the mound was kept low, almost at ground level, in order to capitalize on his sidearm fast ball. Because the mound was so badly defined other Washington pitchers were able to escape detection by the umpires if they edged up a few inches before each pitch.

One day Washington was playing New York—but suppose we let Bucky Harris tell the story the way he once told it to me.

"George Mogridge was pitching for us," said the then manager of the Senators, "and Ruth tagged him for a homer early in the game. Darkness had begun to settle over the field before it ended and the Babe came up in the ninth of a tie ball game. I walked out to Mogridge on the mound.

" 'Don't bother edging up six inches,' I said to him. 'If you're gonna cheat, steal six feet on him.' And that's just what he did."

And what happened then?

"Nothing much," said Harris nonchalantly, "except that the' Babe hit an even longer home run than he had the first time."

Here was a man beyond belief.

Glorious as was his reign as the King of Home Runs, however, there were elements of tragedy in the way he departed from his palace. He was to realize it later and ruefully admit in his autobiography that he never would have done what he did if he had that part of his life to live over again.

The twilight of the gods had come for him in the 1934 season. By baseball standards he was a fat, old man. He hit only twenty-two homers and had a batting average of .288. He insisted on a showdown with Colonel Ruppert. The owner of the Yankees would have to choose between him and Marse Joe McCarthy as manager. Ruppert stuck with McCarthy. So Ruth, getting a quicker release from the Yankees than he ever expected, signed with a shoestring operator, Judge Emil Fuchs of the Boston Braves.

It was disastrous. On opening day there was one Ruthian flare-up. He hit a homer off Carl Hubbell to beat the Giants. Old age had caught up with him, but Judge Fuchs begged him to hang on until the Memorial Day doubleheader.

A few days before that somewhat historic date, the Babe reached back into the past and for a few brief hours captured something of his youth. He hit three home runs in one game against the Pirates.

That's when he should have quit, blazing out.

But he hung on to keep his promise to Judge Fuchs and appeared in the Memorial Day game. After a few innings he limped to the sidelines, the last time that greatest of names was to appear in a box score.

A few days later he sent for Judge Fuchs. Waiting unhappily in the locker room to tell the judge that he'd quit, he saw a troop of reporters come in.

"We're sorry, Babe," one of them said.

"It had to end sometime," said the Babe. "I just had to quit."

"Haven't you heard, Babe?" said another. "You've been fired."

As the Babe was to remark later, "It was quite an ending."

I have one last and personal memory of the Babe. In the summer of 1948 the secret was a secret no longer. Ruth was dying of cancer. The Yankees wanted to do something extra special as a tribute, and so they arranged to retire the King's uniform and number, 3. It would take place at the annual Old-Timers' game and the Bronx Bombers outdid themselves in assembling all the great stars of yesteryear, the Babe's old buddies on the Yankees as well as his friendly enemies from the other teams.

They gathered in the clubhouse, laughing and joking and telling stories. But the man who ordinarily would have been their ringleader in horseplay and in laughter took no part in the proceedings.

It was stiffling hot in that clubhouse. Everyone was sweating as he peeled off his street clothes and climbed into the old uniform he had once worn with such distinction.

Alone in a corner, however, sat the Babe, his massive frame already starting to waste away from the cancer which was to end his life. The Bambino was not only in full uniform but he was wearing a heavy polo coat with the collar turned up. Hot though the room was, he was cold.

Jackie Farrell of the Yankee front office had boxes of shiny new baseballs under his arms.

"Anyone want balls for autographs?" he sang out. He offered one to me.

"Don't be silly, Jackie," I said. "I never got an autograph from a ballplayer in my life."

But when my eye fell on the Babe, I suddenly realized that I might not ever have this opportunity again. I grabbed a ball and walked over to him. He smiled wanly in recognition.

"Would you mind, Babe?" I asked, offering the ball.

"I'd love to, pal," he croaked in a voice that had become strangely muted. In bold strokes he wrote, *Babe Ruth*.

It's the only autographed ball I ever got and I still treasure it. I never spoke to him again.

Not long thereafter he was dead. The body lay in state in the lobby of the Yankee Stadium, "The House That Ruth Built," and 100,000 fans filed past the coffin in sad farewell. With police lines holding back the overflow crowd, the Babe was buried from St. Patrick's Cathedral, at peace with his God at long last.

It rained that day. Even the heavens wept at the passing of Babe Ruth.

3

KING JAMES

Jimmy Foxx

L<small>EFTY</small> GOMEZ knew the trip would be an exhausting one, but his curiosity was so intense that he had to make it anyway. The Singular Señor had just pitched a game for the Yankees against the Philadelphia Athletics at the Stadium and he had seen something he just couldn't believe. He would have to confirm it.

Hurriedly he dressed in the clubhouse behind the dugout, and then he began the long climb upward into the empty stands. He took the ramp to ground level, the ramp to the mezzanine deck and the ramp to the top deck. Then he walked along the passage to the end of the stands adjoining the left-field bullpen before heading up the last set of stairs.

He was gasping for breath as he reached the third row from the top. Then he just gasped. The evidence was unmistakable. The back rung of one seat had been splintered by a violent impact. Lefty knew what had caused it, a baseball he had thrown to James Emory Foxx, the Maryland Strong Boy.

"It's impossible," said the star southpaw. "But old Double-X did it."

Being left-handed, the Singular One even thought in left-handed fashion and eventually grew quite proud of the fact that he had served up what undoubtedly was the longest home run ever produced at the Yankee Stadium, perhaps the hardest-hit ball of all time. It is difficult to say.

47

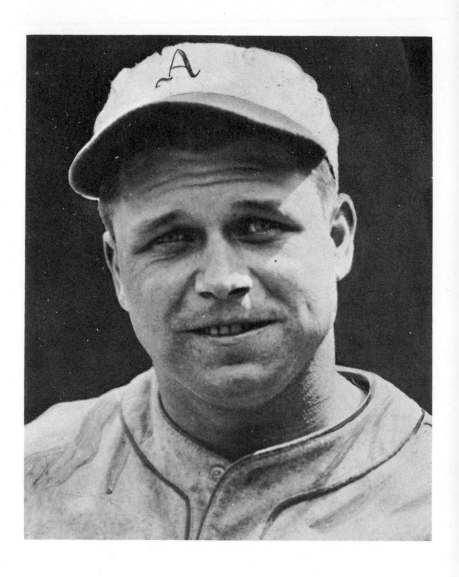

The drive that Foxx crashed that day broke a seat that was three rows from the back of the upper stands. It was about twenty feet in from the edge of the stands. If it had been only some twenty feet to the right, it would have sailed over the bullpen and into the street beyond, the first and only ball ever hit fair out of the Stadium.

That night the excited Gomez was still talking about that prodigious wallop to his roomie, Joe DiMaggio.

"I actually threw the ball half past him," said Lefty. "It was the second half that was too tough. *Wow!*"

Jimmy Foxx was a large and amiable citizen who was known affectionately to his teammates as "The Beast." A solid 200-pounder who was a shade under six feet in height, he was so strong that the other players said of him, "Even his sweat has muscles." He handled a bat as if it were a toy stick in his powerful fists.

The Maryland Strong Boy was, in many respects, a right-handed-hitting Babe Ruth. He had none of the Babe's teeming color or magnetic appeal, but he could hit a ball as far—and frequently did.

Perhaps it's even pointless to say that, if the Babe never had existed, Jimmy Foxx would have been the home run king. Not every baseball fan realizes that Double-X is the crown prince, the runner-up to the Bambino with 527 homers during his twenty-year career.

There was one stretch in that career when he scared the daylights out of the Ruth idolators by smashing fifty-eight home runs in one season, a mark that Hank Greenberg was to match six years later in 1938. When he failed to surpass the Ruthian record of sixty, the least surprised person was Jimmy Foxx.

"I never even had a notion that I might be able to break the Babe's record," he once told me in matter-of-fact fashion. "I injured my wrist in August and I doubt that I

hit three homers during that entire month. Even at that,
though, conditions were different with screens being added
to some ball parks. The Babe's record will be awfully hard
to crack."

Easygoing Jimmy didn't seem the slightest bit perturbed
that architectural rearrangements had ruined his opportunity to shatter a classic record. Yet he had every right
to beef.

On three occasions in his 58-homer year of 1932 he
crashed drives against screens atop fences. Instead of home
runs he got doubles. Twice he hammered out homers at
the start of ball games, games that were washed out by rain
before they lasted long enough to be considered legal.
Down the drain with them went the two homers.

Even those of us who aren't good at arithmetic can figure
out that Double-X lost five might-have-been round-trippers
that season for a might-have-been total of sixty-three. Don't
jump to conclusions, though. Once the magic number of
sixty is approached, the pressures become so enormous
and the overanxious hitters are so completely at the mercy
of uncooperative pitchers that the Ruthian record flits away,
just out of reach. There still is no guarantee that the Maryland Strong Boy would have done the job, even with those
extra five homers.

Foxx was able to outslug the older boys when he was a
160-pound fourteen-year-old along Maryland's Eastern
Shore. Before he had finished high school as a combination
pitcher and third baseman, he'd caught the eye of one of
Connie Mack's old heroes on the Athletics, J. Franklin
Baker, also known as Home Run Baker. There must have
been irony in that discovery because Foxx was to hit as
many homers in one season as the man with the home run
label had smitten in a lifetime. Baker was managing the

Easton club of the Eastern Shore League and was searching for a catcher.

"Do you think you can catch?" he asked the powerfully built seventeen-year old.

"I don't know, sir," said Double-X. "I'm willing to try."

A year later he was with the Athletics and that wasn't the best spot in the sport for a fellow who aspired to be a catcher. The A's already had a catcher. He was Foxx's roommate. His name was Mickey Cochrane and he was the best. So Jimmy did little for a few years except catch batting practice and pinch-hit.

Throughout spring training of 1929 the ancient Mr. Mack used Foxx at third base in an effort to get his big bat in the lineup. Just before opening day that season Baseball's Oldest Inhabitant—Connie Mack was to manage the Athletics until he was eighty-eight years old—approached Jimmy in almost apologetic fashion.

"Jimmy," said the gentle old man. "Do you have a first baseman's mitt?"

"No, sir," said Jimmy.

"Better buy one," said Connie, "because you're our regular first baseman from now on."

Foxx, not yet twenty-two years old, batted .354 with thirty-three home runs as the Athletics, one of the great teams in baseball history, swept to a pennant and a world championship, the first of three successive pennants.

At bat he was a terror. One day the quaint Lefty Gomez was pitching against him. Bill Dickey, his catcher, signaled for a fast ball. Lefty shook him off. Dickey called for a curve. Lefty refused. Finally the big catcher had called for every pitch in the Gomez repertoire. So he stalked to the mound angrily.

"What goes on here?" said Dickey. "I've called for every

pitch you have. What do you want to pitch to this guy?"

"To tell you the truth," said the droll Lefty, "I'd rather not pitch to him at all. I've been stalling out here in the hope that he'd go away."

At one stage in the Gomez career he decided that his eyesight was failing and that he should wear glasses. The experiment was quickly abandoned. But why?

"I was pitching one day," said Lefty, a man whose sense of humor always worked overtime, "when my glasses clouded up on me. I took them off to polish them. When I looked at the plate, I saw Jimmy Foxx. The sight of him terrified me so much that I haven't been able to wear glasses since."

Actually the Singular Señor and Double-X were good enough friends off the playing field to have dinner together occasionally. After the first game of a series with the Athletics at the Stadium, they went out together. One subject was uppermost on Lefty's mind when they met, the remarkable pitching feat of Tommy Bridges of the Tigers that day. "Can you imagine?" said Lefty. "Tommy had a no-hitter going for him with two out in the ninth. Then a pinch hitter breaks it up with a single."

"A lousy break," said Jimmy. "How can anyone be that mean, spoiling a no-hitter?"

"He should be boiled in oil," said Lefty, speaking like a pitcher. "If anyone ever did that to me, I'd kill him."

The next day the artful Lefty spun a one-hitter against the Athletics. Who spoiled his no-hitter? You guessed it— Jimmy Foxx.

In the 1930 World Series between the Athletics and the Cardinals, the opening-day pitcher for the Redbirds from St. Louis was tough Burleigh Grimes, one of the last of the legal spitball operators. Grimes fired in spitter after spitter. In one crucial spot Foxx came to bat. Burleigh came through with spitters for strikes and then bent in a curve. Double-X struck out.

"Gee," he muttered to himself as he walked back to the dugout. "I never knew he threw curves. I just hope he throws me another."

The Series was tied at 2-all when Grimes returned to the mound for the fifth game against George Earnshaw and, for the last two innings, Lefty Grove. It was a scorcher, a scoreless tie into the ninth.

Cochrane opened with a walk. Al Simmons went out and up came the Maryland Strong Boy. Grimes glared at him and remembered something. He brought glove to mouth, faking a spitter. He broke off a curve. Foxx sent it soaring into the left-field bleachers for a home run that won the game, 2 to 0.

That winter the paths of Grimes and Foxx crossed.

"Funny thing about that World Series," mused Burleigh. "I threw only two curve balls in the entire Series, both to you. You fanned on the first and homered on the second."

That ball park in St. Louis was a happy hunting ground for Double-X. In those days the St. Louis Browns shared it with the Cardinals, and the Athletics rolled in for a day that Jimmy long remembered.

In the first game of a doubleheader the Strong Boy crashed out two home runs. In the second game he repeated the operation. But he also added two more majestic smashes, each more than 400 feet in length. Each crashed against the top of the fence. One bounced back on the playing field for a double, the other for a triple. Thus did he come within a couple of feet of slamming six homers in one afternoon.

Although Connie Mack had assembled one of the great teams of baseball history, he soon discovered that they were a luxury he could not afford. His payroll was far too high

for the depression years of the early thirties, and so Connie
Mack, the owner of the team, had to embarrass himself as
manager by selling his stars.

The turn of Double-X came in 1936. The wealthy Tom
Yawkey purchased him for the Red Sox and easygoing
Jimmy found it quite an emotional jolt. But once he settled
down firmly in his surroundings, he found the neighborly
left-field fence a convenient target area. In 1938 he slammed
fifty homers, batted .349 and was elected Most Valuable
Player in the American League for the third time. He'd
previously won in 1932 and 1933.

But he slipped faster than all those muscles and all that
strength had indicated. His enormous willingness to play
any position in his early years sped up his departure. It
came in 1942 when he was only thirty-four. He was waived
to the Cubs, drifted to the minors and was rescued by the
Phils during the wartime manpower shortages of 1945. By
now he was the complete handyman.

One day Ben Chapman, manager of the Phils, came to
him.

"Jimmy," he said. "We're desperate. Would you mind
getting yourself in shape to pitch? We don't have anyone
who can get the ball over the plate."

"I couldn't go nine innings under any conditions," said
the Maryland Strong Boy. "I'm not even sure I could get
anyone out."

"Just hang in there as long as you can," begged Chapman. "If, by some miracle, you could last five innings,
that's all I'll ask. I'll take you right out."

It was a promise that could not be kept and the fellow
who prevented it was Double-X himself. He was too good.
He pitched against the Cincinnati Reds and at the end of
five innings he was pitching a no-hitter. Chapman left
him in.

In the sixth inning Jimmy's arm was as dead as a dinosaur and he felt just as heavy. The Reds nicked him for a hit and that was one hint Chapman could not overlook. He yanked Foxx while he still was a winning pitcher and brought in a reliever to preserve the victory.

It was to be the last appearance of James Emory Foxx in a major league box score. There is a touch of irony in that very item.

Babe Ruth, the king, began his big league career as a pitcher. Jimmy Foxx, the crown prince, ended his on that identical note.

4

KING THEODORE

Ted Williams

THE Boston Red Sox had just lost a game they had no right to lose. They had dropped a squeaker on a couple of flukes and they were so mad that they wouldn't even talk to each other, much less to strangers. And the strangers awaited outside, a mob of fans on the sidewalk. They left a narrow lane from clubhouse door to the bus which was to take the Bosox to the airport.

The angry players were so blinded with rage that they didn't see the autograph hounds. If they saw them, they ignored them as they brushed through into the bus. And then came Ted Williams, just as mad as the rest of them. Impatiently he shook off the pesky fans and leaped for the bus door. Suddenly he stopped.

"Will you help me, Ted?" said a trembling little voice.

"What do you want, kid?" said Ted, voice harsh but eyes soft. The boy was crippled and was holding an autograph book. Williams snatched it and jumped into the bus.

"Listen, you baboons," he bellowed. "Everybody sign."

The Great Man went down the aisle, collecting autographs from every member of the squad. He walked back to the door of the bus and shoved the book at the boy.

"Here, kid," growled Ted. "Now beat it."

He waited for no thanks. But he got them nonetheless in the ecstatically happy look of the proudest and most grateful little boy in Boston.

Theodore Samuel Williams is a strange one. His personality is so complex that even high-powered psychiatrists would have trouble in finding out what makes him tick. He can charm a bird out of a tree or he can antagonize people, depending on his mood. If he had not been so stubborn, he could have won over those fans who rode him unmercifully. He wouldn't even try.

But one section of the populace which thought he was the greatest was the young. Ted never was able to resist the kids and his love for children was genuine. There's no way of calculating the good he did for the Jimmy Fund, an organization whose objective is the conquering of leukemia, a cancer of the blood which strikes down children. He has been the spearhead of a drive which has raised hundreds of thousands of dollars for hospitalization and research. And his visits to hospital wards were as frequent as they were unpublicized.

The glorious Williams career has ended and it ended without his reaching a goal he set in his rookie year.

"All I want out of life," he said dreamily, "is to be able to walk down the street and have people point at me and say, 'There goes the greatest hitter that ever lived.' "

He came close but he didn't quite attain it. Part of it was due to his own stubbornness and part of it was due to his misfortune of losing five of his most productive years as an aviator in the Marine Corps. Three of those lost seasons came during World War II when he was reaching an early peak as a twenty-four-year old. The other two came for the Korean war just as he'd leveled off as a knowledgeable thirty-two-year old.

Among other things, it cost him certain runner-up honors to Babe Ruth in the all-time home run derby. As it was, he completed his career with 521 homers, just thirteen short of Jimmy Foxx's runner-up figure of 534. Give Williams back the five lost years and he would have had approximately 670 homers, not too far behind the Babe's wondrous 714.

His lifetime average also was watered down by the five missing years even though he did finish with a handsome .344. Still outranking him among the moderns are Ty Cobb with .367, Rogers Hornsby with .358, Shoeless Joe Jackson with .356 and Lefty O'Doul with .349.

Not since the Shoeless One has baseball had a finer natural hitter than the Boston Strong Boy. And not since Cobb has the game had a more dedicated student of the art of hitting. Ted studied every pitcher and every hitter he saw. He discussed batting for hour after endless hour with every great hitter he encountered—Cobb, Hornsby and all the rest.

Nor did he ever withhold this immense store of knowledge from any ballplayer who sought it, friend and foe alike. After Al Kaline had won the American League batting championship, I kiddingly asked him what was the secret of his success.

"Ted Williams," he said. "His advice straightened me out."

Rocky Colavito, then with the Indians, came to Fenway Park one day while in the grip of a dreadful slump. Immediately he sought out Williams for help. Then Rocky beat the Bosox with two home runs.

"I don't object to Ted's generosity with his advice," quipped one Bostonian afterward. "But I wish he wouldn't overdo it."

Williams had a swing that was flawless, the perfect batting swing. Whenever he stepped into the cage for batting practice, other ballplayers paid him the supreme tribute. They paused in whatever they were doing and watched. Only Babe Ruth commanded such respect and admiration.

Ted was good and he knew it. He always knew it. That's

what caused him so much trouble in the beginning. Although he was a pitcher in high school in San Diego, his hitting ability made him an outfielder whenever he wasn't on the mound. In that capacity he joined the San Diego Padres of the Pacific Coast League under Frank Shellenbach.

The debut of the seventeen-year-old Williams as a pitcher was somewhat noteworthy. The Padres were being soundly beaten when Shellenbach sent in the kid for the final two innings. He got by the first of those innings all right, but in the next one he was greeted by single, double, single and home run. Shellenbach hastened from the dugout.

"Look," said Ted, a compulsive talker when things are at their worst. "There's no one on base."

"No one on base?" said the incredulous manager. "Are you screwy?"

"No," said Ted cheerfully, "but you ought to be able to see by now that as a pitcher I'm a pretty good outfielder."

It was as an outfielder that he was spotted by Eddie Collins while on an inspection tour for the Red Sox.

"How could I miss?" said Collins afterward. "Williams stood out like a brown cow in a pasture of white cows."

Acting tough and talking tough, Ted reported the next spring to the training camp at Sarasota, hiding his uncertainty behind a mask of bravado. He talked back to everyone.

"Wait until you see Jimmy Foxx hit," said Bobby Doerr, Ted's onetime teammate at San Diego.

"Wait until Foxx sees me hit," said Williams loudly. He meant it, too.

Ted was always practicing batting, even when he was in the outfield. He kept swinging at imaginary pitches with an imaginary bat. Among those he irritated was Joe Cronin, the manager and shortstop.

"Hey, busher," Cronin called out in the middle of an exhibition game. "Why not practice this?" He went through the motions of a man fielding a ground ball.

Cronin stood as much of Williams as he could and then sent him to the Minneapolis Millers of the American Association. Among those members of the Red Sox who bade him farewell were the three regular outfielders, Ben Chapman, Doc Cramer and Joe Vosmik.

"So long, busher," they jeered.

"I'll be back, you no-good baboons," roared Williams, "and someday I'll be earning more dough than the three of you combined."

He would do precisely that, too.

At Minneapolis the exiled busher delighted the fans with his hitting but dismayed them with his fielding. Actually he was not a bad fielder. He had a strong arm, was faster than he looked and judged a ball well—provided he was paying attention and not swinging that imaginary bat. Donie Bush, the manager, took all he could and then stormed into the office of Mike Kelley, the owner of the team.

"Mike," he said. "I can't take it any more. This place isn't big enough for Williams and me. One of us has to go."

"I wouldn't be that rash, Donie," said Mike. "If an owner has to choose between his manager and a .370 hitter, you should be able to guess which one he'd pick."

So Williams stayed. So did Bush. By the season's end Ted led the Association in batting with .366 and in homers with forty-three. The Red Sox traded off Chapman, a .340 hitter, to make room for him. Nor did Ted disappoint. As a rookie he batted .327, had thirty-one homers and 145 runs batted in. A year later he was up to .344 and in 1941 was ready for the greatest season of his remarkable career.

He started fast and never slowed down. By the time of the All-Star game he was pulverizing all pitching for a .405

average. And in the ninth inning of that midsummer classic, with two on and two out, he hit a prodigious homer into the upper right-field deck to win the game.

Pressures grew steadily more intense as the campaign moved along and Ted was still over the .400 mark. He was equal to it, though, until the final week when he wavered a bit. Going into the final day, he saw his average ease off to .39955. In accordance with baseball practice and tradition those figures are translated into .400.

What to do? Should he play it safe and accept his technical .400? Or should he risk everything by playing?

"Better sit it out, kid," advised Manager Joe Cronin.

"No," said Ted. "If I'm going to be the champion, I want to win like a champion. I'm playing."

He merely made six hits in eight times at bat for an average of .406. Handsome is as handsome does.

He thus became the first .400 batsman since Bill Terry of the Giants in 1930 and the first American Leaguer since Harry Heilmann in 1923. Nor has anyone come close to him since.

The following season of 1942 was a troubled year for him. The United States was at war and Williams was young, strong and healthy. But he also was tough-minded and stubborn. He'd started at a rookie's salary and 1942 was to be his first big money year at $30,000. Desperately he wanted that money, not for himself but for a widowed mother whose sole support he was. He asked for a draft deferment and got it. Critical mail rolled in by the bagful.

That May the big fellow sneaked quietly off and enlisted in the air arm of the Marines, hoping he wouldn't be called before the season's end. Typically enough, he insisted on no publicity.

His mind at ease, he went back to baseball and captured that rare prize, the Triple Crown—batting champion at

.356, homer champion at thirty-six and runs-batted-in champion at 137.

So off he went to the Marines who confirmed a fact that every American League pitcher had long suspected. Examining doctors discovered that his eyesight had a sharpness such as they find only once in a hundred thousand. It has been said of him that he can identify a duck on the wing long before most people can even spot the duck.

It was natural that Ted would be an exceptional pilot. He was so competent that he was held on as an instructor and by the time he reached the combat zone the war was over.

When Williams returned to baseball, a new batting star had entered the American League, Dick Wakefield of Detroit, a colorful and likable guy. He challenged Williams to all sorts of bets as to which would have the higher batting average, more homers and everything else. Commissioner Chandler frowned on this and ordered the bets canceled. The next spring I mentioned it to Ted.

"Those were silly bets," he told me in matter-of-fact fashion. "Wakefield never was in my class as a hitter."

It almost was a shocking statement. Yet this wasn't a boastful man talking. The world's foremost authority on hitting was merely giving an impersonal and measured appraisal of a situation as he saw it. He was absolutely right, too. Wakefield never was in his class as a hitter.

This was the year, however, when something happened which was to chop perhaps twenty to thirty points off the Williams lifetime average. Lou Boudreau, the manager of the Cleveland Indians, invented his satanic Boudreau Shift.

Being a left-handed pull hitter, Williams hammered most of his shots to right. That was his power zone. So the deep-thinking Boudreau moved all four of his infielders to the right of second base and placed two of his three outfielders there, leaving only his left fielder to guard the entire left side of the field. This shift or variations of it were adopted by every team in the American League and also by Eddie Dyer, manager of the St. Louis Cardinals, for the World Series against the Red Sox.

A student of human nature, Boudreau knew exactly how Ted would react to the shift. Ted would not sidestep and hit to left. His stubbornness demanded that he meet it head on, bulling his way to right.

During the World Series in St. Louis a couple of visitors dropped in on Ted in his room in the Chase Hotel, Grantland Rice and myself. We spent a couple of hours in good-natured argument.

"You can defeat that shift instantly, Ted," said his journalistic friends, "by bunting or slicing everything to left. No team can afford to give away that much. They'll have to return their defenses to normal."

"They're trying to make me hit singles to left," said Ted, white with rage. "And I won't give in to them. I won't let them take the home run away from me. The only way to defeat the shift is to overpower it."

By the third game of the World Series the Boston Strong Boy was so hungry for hits that he dumped a bunt down the third base line. Boston newspapers have always been aware of the fact that Williams is their most newsworthy figure. The next day one paper used an eight-column scare headline on its front page, the kind that normally is reserved for the declaration of war or the election of a President. It read:

WILLIAMS BUNTS SAFELY

Ted had an indifferent World Series, the only post-season play of his career. He batted .200. The shift bothered him

far more than he ever would admit. Ted's stubborn reaction
to it left Ty Cobb aghast and Ty told me about it when
I next saw him.

"If they had used that shift against me," said baseball's greatest batsman, "I would have batted a thousand.
I'd have stopped it fast by hitting everything to left. You're
a friend of Ted's. Tell him what I said when you next see
him."

Ted was told. It made no difference. Yet if he ever had
paused to think how the pennant-clinching game was won
in 1946, he might have reconsidered. He's a highly intelligent man but on this one phase of the sport he had a complete blind spot.

For the better part of a week, the Fenway Millionaires
had been trying to clinch the flag. Then in late September
they tangled with the Indians in a scorcher. Into the ninth
inning they rolled in a scoreless tie. Up stepped Theodore
Samuel Williams and sliced one to left against weakened
defenses. The ball rolled to the fence and Ted had the first
and only inside-the-park homer of his career. It won the
game, 1 to 0, and clinched the pennant.

One reason Ted carried on so many feuds was because he
had what the trade calls "rabbit ears." He heard every un-
complimentary remark ever made.

"I realized what an artist Ted is with a bat," Cronin told
me one day, "when some blabbermouth in the stands gave
him an unmerciful riding. Ted was spouting sparks when he
came to the dugout.

" 'There's a fathead in left,' he howled, 'who's been riding
my pants off. The next time I get to bat I'm gonna smack
that big mouth right between the eyes with a foul ball.'

"He fouled the first pitch and made leatherlungs duck.
So I kept count. Ted fouled seventeen balls at that guy and
he never was more than six feet from the target."

Certainly it was childish. But he despised the fair-weather fans who booed him one moment and gave him resounding cheers whenever he would hit a home run. So he always refused to tip his cap to the applauding multitudes when he crossed the plate and headed toward the dugout.

"If he'd just tip his cap once," said Eddie Collins sadly, "he could be elected mayor of Boston in five minutes. I don't think he'll ever do it."

On a homeward-bound train one day, three teammates went to work on him, Birdie Tebbetts, Bobby Doerr and Dom DiMaggio.

"You could be as popular as Babe Ruth," said Birdie. "He had the fans eating out of his hand because he always acknowledged their cheers by tipping his hat."

"It's the only polite and decent thing to do," said Bobby.

"Try it just once," urged Dom. "The response of the fans will make you pleased that you did it."

Reluctantly Ted agreed. On his next home run he'd tip his hat. The next day rain washed out the game. A day later the three conspirators sat in the dugout as Ted went to bat.

"Think he'll do it?" said Doerr.

"If we'd played yesterday," said the shrewd Tebbetts, "I think he would have. But this extra day has given him more time to think about it."

Williams swung. The ball sailed on a majestic arc toward the right-field bullpen. The three edged forward on the bench. Ted took a couple of uncertain steps down the first base line, torn by an inner struggle. Then he almost stopped as he turned toward the dugout.

"I can't do it," he shouted. "I just can't do it."

Just as the Williams career was moving along nicely the second call to duty came. The Marines called him back for the Korean war, a headline-catching device which hardly was fair to Ted. He was then thirty-three years old and 220 pounds of solid muscle was now packed on the six-foot four-inch frame of a man Bostonians once had called the Splendid Splinter. So remarkable are his reflexes, though, that he soon was flying jet fighter planes.

On his way back from a massive raid over North Korea the big Marine captain made an unhappy discovery; a lot of them, in fact. His radio didn't work; his ailerons were stuck; his airspeed indicator was gone and flames were blazing from his brake ports. Any other pilot would have bailed out. But Ted thrives on challenges. He brought in his Panther jet in a belly landing, saving the plane. He wasn't scratched.

He returned to the Red Sox in midsummer of 1953, worked out furiously and made his second pinch-hitting try on August 10. All he did was drill a 400-footer into the bleachers in right center for a home run.

"Ted has set back spring training twenty years," said a grinning Joe Cronin.

When he was thirty-eight years old this remarkable man batted .388 and had thirty-eight homers. A year later he edged out his teammate and prize pupil, Pete Runnels, for the batting championship, his sixth and last. He was forty-two when he quit in 1960 and he departed on a high note that was in keeping with his character. He batted .317 and slammed twenty-nine homers.

Unlike Ruth who played just a couple of games too many for a drab and anticlimactic exit, Ted went out with a grand flourish. It was as perfect as if a Hollywood scriptwriter had penned the lines for him. In his last at bat in Fenway Park he crashed a titanic home run.

"That's the end," said Ted sadly. "There's nothing more I can do."

There wasn't either. What he had accomplished, he'd done wonderfully well.

5

KING MELVIN

Mel Ott

MEL OTT was about to start his fifth season as a member of the New York Giants, a glamour team that was run by the most glamorous figure in the game, the dynamic John McGraw. Master Melvin walked briskly into the hotel dining room at spring training, a look of mischief in his eye.

Spotting McGraw at breakfast, he approached the hot-tempered manager of the Giants.

"Mister McGraw," said Ottie respectfully. "There was a man in my room this morning."

"Who?" thundered the Little Napoleon.

"Me," said the twinkle-eyed youth. "I'm twenty-one years old today."

Perhaps nothing better illustrates what an unusual person Master Melvin was. Before he even had reached voting age, he had been a big-leaguer for four years and had attained acclaim as one of the great stars of his day.

He was unusual in another respect, his size. He was a compact little powerhouse who stood only five feet nine and weighed only 170 pounds. But only three men ever hit more home runs than did the darling of the Polo Grounds clientele—Babe Ruth, Jimmy Foxx and Ted Williams. All were huge, brawny men. And all, oddly enough, were American Leaguers.

So this handsome little boy was to emerge as the home run king of the National League with a total of 511, the

fourth and last member of the exclusive Five Hundred Club.
Destiny directed him to the Polo Grounds and to John Mc-
Graw, the perfect combination for his unique talents.

It is doubtful that baseball ever produced a more likable
or popular performer than the Little Giant. He even drew
cheers in Brooklyn where those rabid Dodger fans booed
enemy players with such violence that they cringed from
the assault on their eardrums. But Ottie was extra special.
In fact, he's the only baseball man who ever was publicly
characterized as a "nice guy," in an incident which has since
become part of Americana.

It happened in 1946 when Leo Durocher was managing
the Dodgers with all of his brassy arrogance and skill. Ottie
was managing the Giants and not too well. When the Brooks
came into the Polo Grounds for a series, they were in first
place and the Giants were dragging along in the cellar.

Leo the Lip was yapping away in the dugout before the
game, making cruel jests at the less fortunate. He was in
great form. One newspaperman, Frank Graham, stood as
much as he could and then spoke up.

"Why are you so nasty, Leo?" he asked. "Why don't you
try to be a nice guy?"

Durocher snorted derisively and jerked his thumb contemptuously in the direction of Ottie in the opposite dugout.

"Who wants to be a nice guy?" he said, spitting out the
words. "Nice guys finish last."

If Ottie wasn't cut out to be a great manager, he was cut
out to be a great ballplayer, and this was one instance
where a nice guy kept finishing up near the top. There even
was one stage in the history of the Giants when the hitting
of Master Melvin and the pitching of his roommate, Carl
Hubbell, were the main reasons the club remained in con-
tention. After the weight of their years swept them to the

sidelines, the club faltered so dreadfully that the situation was satirized in the Baseball Writers Show in this fashion:

> *A Giant is a midget, gettin' by on his past.*
> *He can't hit a hook or nuthin' fast.*
> *The club makes money but it's gone to pot.*
> *The fans go there to dream of Hubbell and Ott.*

One of the secrets of McGraw's success as a manager was that he had a legion of friends scattered throughout the country and they were continually tipping him off on hot prospects. This, of course, was long before each ball club organized its own army of scouts to honeycomb the land. One of the Little Napoleon's buddies was Harry Williams, a wealthy lumberman from New Orleans.

Just before sailing for Europe in the summer of 1925, Williams told McGraw about a sixteen-year-old catcher from nearby Gretna, Louisiana, who was playing on the semipro team that Williams sponsored, a kid named Melvin Thomas Ott. He told McGraw but he forgot to tell Ottie. So he hastily scrawled a message on a postcard.

Report immediately to John McGraw at the Polo Grounds, said the postcard.

"People shouldn't make jokes about so serious a matter," said Master Melvin, failing to recognize the almost indecipherable signature. He threw the card away.

Williams was horrified to find Ottie in Louisiana when he returned from Europe in September. Immediately he sent the boy, cardboard suitcase and all, to New York. Mel got lost in the subway after he arrived but finally reached the Polo Grounds. Timidly he approached the office of the man he was to idolize. Clutching the handle of his suitcase in one feverish hand, he knocked on the door with the other.

"Come in!" roared a voice.

Master Melvin tried hard to keep the tremble from his

voice as he blurted out a greeting which was to mark the start of an amazing career.

"Mister McGraw, I'm Mel Ott," he announced.

The little sixteen-year-old caught batting practice and did odd chores during the few weeks left of the season. But he got in no games. It really wasn't until spring training that McGraw was able to give him a thorough appraisal.

One day Mel was catching when he noticed McGraw engrossed in a deep discussion with Roger Bresnahan, the Hall of Famer who coached the catchers. Instinctively, Master Melvin knew he was the topic of their conversation and a wild fear surged through him. Desperately he yearned to stay with the Giants but he was terrified that he would be sent out to the minors. McGraw beckoned to him.

"Have you ever done anything but catch?" he asked.

"Yes, Mister McGraw," bravely answered the boy. "I used to play the outfield *when I was a kid.*"

The farseeing McGraw had noticed that the baby-faced youngster had unusually heavy legs. Constant crouching behind the plate would make them increasingly muscle-bound. Ottie wouldn't last ten years as a catcher. The Little Napoleon shrewdly switched the boy to the outfield. That was Ott's first big break.

The second came when McGraw studied a batting style which had a peculiar leg hitch. As Ottie stepped into the pitch with his left-handed swing, he raised his right or forward foot off the ground and stabbed ahead with it. So unorthodox was this mannerism that every manager in the business—except McGraw—would have changed it.

After Ottie had been with the Giants for a full season, the team headed north from spring training and paused in Memphis where Tom Watkins tossed a birthday party for the dynamic skipper of the Giants. All baseball men in the vicinity were invited, including a guy who was just starting his own managerial career, a certain Casey Stengel of the Toledo Mudhens.

The Ol' Perfessor was as wily then as he was to prove later on. He waited until the party had reached its height and McGraw was in a most expansive and generous mood. Then he approached his old boss.

"Mac," said Casey, "I was just thinkin' I might help you by takin' some of them young kids off your hands and playin' them regular for me whilst I teach 'em a few things. Now if I could have that kid, Mel Ott . . ."

McGraw exploded in one angry outburst.

"Never," he screamed. "I'm not letting you or any other clown of a minor league manager ruin that boy. He has the best natural swing I've seen in years and I don't want it changed. I'm keeping him myself."

That's why Ottie never played in the minors and never played for any team except the Giants during his twenty-two years as a major-leaguer, most of them glorious ones. Throughout all those early years McGraw watched over the boy with the gruff tenderness of a strict but loving father. On one trip he spotted Master Melvin in the club car, playing poker with Bill Terry and other veterans.

"That will cost you a $100 fine," growled McGraw. "You're too young to be playing cards with grown men."

Once the Little Napoleon levied a fine, it stuck. He never canceled it or returned the money. But the soft streak of the hard-boiled Giant manager frequently impelled him to do the same thing in a left-handed way. The next day Mel hit a home run of no importance or significance. Awaiting him in his locker was McGraw's personal check for $100, a bonus for nothing.

Sparingly the Giant skipper used his infant prodigy that first season of 1926. Ottie broke into only thirty-five games but he hit .383, not a bad average for a seventeen-year-old

boy. A year later he was in twice as many games and hit
the first of his 511 homers. It was the only one he hit that
season, too.

"I'm almost ashamed to tell you about it," the modest
hero once said to me. "I hit a low line drive over second
base. Hack Wilson came racing in from center field to try
for a shoestring catch. He slipped on the wet turf and the
ball rolled all the way to the fence. So my first one was an
inside-the-park homer."

Twenty years later he made his last, an opening-day shot
off Oscar Judd of the Phillies. It was the only homer he was
to smash during part-time service over the final two cam-
paigns as an active player.

During the first few seasons McGraw insisted that Ott
sit at his side whenever he was in the dugout, and the Old
Master filled his head with knowledge. Physical errors he
ignored but McGraw would get wrathful at mental errors.
One afternoon in his first season, Ottie pulled a beauty.

Freddie Lindstrom was on first base when Master Melvin
lined a shot to right. Lindy had to hold up to make certain
that the ball would not be caught. Then he jogged to second.
But Ottie knew it wouldn't be caught and he was sure he
had an easy double. He slid beautifully into second in a
cloud of dust. The dust settled. Ottie looked up to see
Lindstrom standing on the bag and laughing at him.

"Great slide, kid," said Lindy. "But one of us is gonna
be out."

When Ott was twenty years old, he batted .328 and had
forty-two home runs. He might have had a tie for the home
run championship with Chuck Klein of the Phils but sportsmanship was absent at Baker Bowl that day.

"They ganged up on me," sadly commented Master Melvin many years later. They sure did.

In the first game of a doubleheader the Boy Wonder was

held to a single while Klein belted one off Carl Hubbell for
his forty-third. Then the Phils slammed the door in Ott's
face. They made it absolutely impossible for him to tie
Klein.

In the first inning of the second game he was given four
wide ones for a walk he didn't want. In the third he lunged
at what was supposed to be a fourth ball and accidentally
made a single. He was walked in the fourth, sixth and
eighth innings of what had become a ridiculously one-sided
game in favor of the Giants.

The ninth inning arrived and Ottie was the seventh
scheduled hitter which meant he had no chance to get a
last swing at the fences. But with two on and two out Doc
Farrell singled, Pat Crawford scratched an infield dribbler
and the bases were full with Master Melvin stepping buoy-
antly to bat.

No longer would the Phillies be able to walk him. It was
the ninth inning, the bases were full and the Giants were
winning, 11 to 3. But the Phillies flouted all laws of common sense and sportsmanship. Fidgety Phil Collins, the
pitcher, received orders to walk the hitter. Klein's championship must be protected at all costs.

Three wide ones whisked outside the plate, Ottie getting
madder and madder. As a fourth ball came whistling in,
Mel swung at it anyway and missed for a strike. He did
it again. But the next one gave him free passage as a run
was forced in. Then Master Melvin completed the bur-
lesque in disdainful fashion. He let himself get picked off
the bag to end the inning.

But if fate played a scurvy trick on him then, that same
fickle lass made amends eight years later in 1937. At the
season's end two men were tied for the home run title at
thirty-one each, Joe Medwick of the Cardinals and Mel
Ott of the Giants. But the muscleman from St. Louis had

belted one into the seats in the first inning one rainy afternoon, a perfectly legitimate home run.

But it lost its legitimacy when a heavy downpour washed
out the game before it had reached the four-and-a-half-
inning minimum. Washed out with it were all runs, hits,
errors, strikeouts, walks—and Medwick's homer. So they
wound up in a tie, one of the six times that Master Melvin
won or shared the home run championship.

One time he even had to share a home run with McGraw
—at least the manager took part credit, in an unexpected
burst of good humor. But the Little Napoleon had set that
up by his inflexible insistence on iron discipline.

The Giants were a couple of runs behind one afternoon
with runners on base and with Ottie, the powerhouse of the
team, the next hitter. Master Melvin glanced over for the
signal and was so shocked he backed out of the batter's
box for a second look. He still couldn't believe it. So he
picked up a handful of dirt, rubbed it on his hands and
stared a third time. There could be no mistaking it. Mc-
Graw had given the sign for a bunt.

The Boy Wonder dropped down so neat a bunt that the
confused enemy was caught out of position. He had a hit
and all runners were safe to trigger a rally that won the
game. Ottie was peeling off his uniform in the clubhouse
afterward when McGraw stampeded over, fire in his eye.

"Don't you dare question my strategy again," roared
McGraw.

"I didn't say a word, Mister McGraw," said Mel.

"No," screamed McGraw, "but I didn't like the questions
in your eyes."

It was only a few days later when Mel stepped to bat
again. Once more there were runners on base and the Giants
were two runs behind. The pitcher was wild and served up
three balls. Baseball tradition ordains that the batter take

the next pitch without swinging. He lets the "cripple" slide past.

But when Ottie glanced for the sign, he accepted orders without letting any questioning look enter his eyes. McGraw had daringly given the signal to hit. So Master Melvin stroked a screamer over the bullpen wall for a home run that won the game.

"You feel pretty good about that, don't you?" said a smiling McGraw in the clubhouse.

"Yes, sir," he said, "I do."

"I'll share the credit with you," said the pleased skipper in an uncharacteristic flash of humor. "If I hadn't ordered you to hit the cripple, you wouldn't have had the homer. I'm entitled to at least two bases."

"Yes, sir," said Melvin, who knew that the box score would show all four bases for Melvin Thomas Ott.

One of Ottie's deepest regrets was that he never played in the World Series for the man he idolized so much that he always referred to him as "Mister McGraw." By the time Master Melvin made the post-season classic in 1933 against the Senators, Bill Terry was managing the Giants.

The night before the Series opened in Washington, Ottie tossed and twisted in bed, so overwhelmed by excitement that he couldn't sleep. Then he noticed that his roomie, Hughie Critz, couldn't sleep, either. The second baseman finally stood by the window, staring into the blackness and gnawing his fingernails.

"Nervous, Hughie?" asked Mel.

"Shucks, no," drawled Hughie, the Mississippian. "I been waitin' a long time for this and I'm not the least bit worried. Are you?"

"Naw," drawled Mel, the Louisianian, with a forced laugh. "Just another ball game."

Suddenly Mel sat up in bed.

"Know what, Hughie?" he said. "We're a couple of dog-gone liars. Now that we've admitted it, let's get some sleep."

The Giants won the World Series in the tenth inning of the last game. The score was tied, 3 to 3, when the nervous Mr. Ott untied it with a home run.

This power-packed little dynamo had a great flair for the dramatic. One year he found that Frank Watts, a Philadelphia pitcher, had become his favorite pigeon. Every time Watts pitched, Ottie tagged him for at least one homer.

It got to be the final day of the season. In fact it was the eighth inning of the final game and Watts made a discovery. He had completely handcuffed the Little Giant.

"Here's your last chance, Mel," he taunted as Ottie stepped to bat. He slipped past two strikes and the taunting grew louder. He couldn't slip past the third one, though. Mel crashed a whistling drive to deepest right and he began to tear around the bases. When Mel whipped by second, Watts looked toward his pursuing outfielders and began to get alarmed.

"You lucky stiff," he screamed at Ottie. Then he began to run alongside of him, screaming more imprecations. Master Melvin was laughing so hard that he hardly had the strength to slide over the plate with an inside-the-park homer.

The appointment of Ott as Giant manager in 1942 by Horace Stoneham was a mistake. The onetime Boy Wonder was temperamentally unsuited for the job. As a ballplayer he had been immensely popular with his mates. Not only did he have charm and personality, but he spiced it with a mischievous sense of humor. Managers cannot be palsy-walsy with their players and whenever Ottie was forced to crack down on his old buddies, they resented it because it was entirely contrary to his character.

When the ax fell in midseason of 1948, it landed in the cruelest manner possible. Replacing Ottie was awkward enough but the guy who replaced him was the fellow who openly claimed he'd rather be nasty than nice, Leo Durocher, a hated exile from hated Brooklyn.

To the outer world, Master Melvin accepted the blow like the wonderful guy he was. Only those closest to him, though, knew how deep the cut was.

"I'm going to tell you something in confidence," he said to me one time. "I was never so shocked or hurt in my life. As soon as I left the press conference I rushed to the phone to tell my wife. I was calm and almost reconciled to it when I began to talk. But she started to cry and the first thing I knew was that I was crying, too. We blubbered into that phone like a couple of babies."

What has broken the seal of confidence was Mel's sudden death in 1958. By then he had been elected to the Hall of Fame at Cooperstown and had made a huge success as a baseball broadcaster in Detroit. A new and richer life had begun for him.

After the season ended he went to dinner with his wife one evening at a roadhouse just across the Mississippi border and not far from his home in a New Orleans suburb. The swank dining establishment is located on a main highway that frequently is enveloped in fog.

Out of that fog came death. As Master Melvin and his wife steered gropingly onto the road a speeding car crashed into them in a head-on collision. One of the best-loved figures in the world of sports was gone.

But the legend of Mel Ott will long endure, the nice guy who represented everything fine and decent in sports, an inspiration for every small boy and every grown man.

6

KING LOUIS

Lou Gehrig

Every time Paul Krichell, the demon Yankee scout, rode past New Brunswick, N. J., on a Pennsylvania Railroad train, he performed the same ritual. He doffed his hat and bowed reverently in the direction of the baseball field at Rutgers University. That was the place where Krich made the greatest discovery of his distinguished career. That's where he first saw Lou Gehrig.

It was strictly an accident. The eagle scout of the Bronx Bombers had intended to inspect some hot prospect in upstate New York. But Ed Barrow, the general manager of the Yankees, canceled the trip and Krich was left with a free afternoon. He studied the college baseball schedules and the only game was one between Columbia and Rutgers at New Brunswick. Mainly because he had nothing else to do, the scout took it in.

The broad-shouldered, broad-beamed Gehrig had gained more fame as a plunging Columbia fullback than he had as a combination pitcher-outfielder on the baseball team. But he hit the ball with such power that the Yankee scout was goggle-eyed. He still was in a daze when he reported to Barrow the next morning.

"I saw another Babe Ruth today," said Krich, awe in his voice.

Barrow laughed at him.

"Everybody's finding another Ruth," scoffed Barrow.

Krichell didn't argue with him. No one ever dared argue with Barrow.

But a few days later the chief talent inspector made another report.

"I saw Gehrig again today," he said. "He pitched against Penn. But when he came to bat, he not only hit one out of South Field but he knocked the ball all the way up the library steps on the other side of the street. I'm right. He's another Ruth."

By this time even Barrow had become impressed. A speculative gleam entered his eye.

"Can you get him?" asked Ed.

"I already have," said Krich. "He'll be in the office in the morning."

Gehrig signed, reporting at the completion of the school year in June of 1923. The Yankees were at batting practice when tiny Miller Huggins escorted the huge but shy Gehrig out on the field. They formed an incongruous, ill-matched pair. The players snickered.

"Whatcha got there, Hug—Zbyszko?" said one. Zbyszko was the wrestling champion and supposedly the biggest, strongest man in the world. Gehrig blushed. He was big, clumsy and ungainly. He almost seemed out of place among the athletes. Even the Babe, big as he was, moved with a catlike grace.

"Let the kid hit, Joe," said Huggins to Jumping Joe Dugan who was about to enter the batting cage. Dugan stepped aside.

Gehrig reached down blindly and grabbed a bat that was lying alongside the cage. By some curious chance it was Ruth's bat. The ballplayers crowded around the cage, grinning in amusement and derision. In effect they were challenging this mountain of muscle to show them something. Their jeering attitudes demonstrated that they expected nothing.

Larrupin' Lou nervously squeezed the bat until—in ballplayers' language—"the sawdust came out." Then he swung. There was a white streak as the ball went whistling deeply into the right-field bleachers. The Yankees gasped and eyed the big kid with new respect. No one but Ruth had ever hit one that far. Gehrig hit another and another and another.

"That's enough," said Huggins. He turned to the players. "His name is Gehrig," he said.

After riding the bench to get the feel of the big leagues, the Iron Horse—that nickname had yet to be earned—was optioned out to Hartford in the Eastern League. The dictatorial Barrow issued orders to Paddy O'Connor, the manager there, that Gehrig was to be used exclusively and regularly at first base. In no time at all O'Connor was in despair.

"What a stiff they gave me!" he moaned. "That big lug can't hit, can't field, can't do anything."

On the Friday before Labor Day the awkward novice had a batting average of .062. Furthermore, the manager had a far better first baseman sitting on the bench. So he sent Barrow a wire, pleading for permission to abandon the Gehrig project as hopeless. But luck was with Larrupin' Lou. The telegram lay unopened on Barrow's desk over the long Labor Day weekend.

Although O'Connor knew that his request would be granted, he still didn't dare make the move without a specific okay. So he was stuck with Gehrig. On Saturday Lou won a game with a home run. On Sunday he broke up both games of a doubleheader with thunderous hits and O'Connor was beginning to say enthusiastically, "I knew that kid had the makings of a great hitter."

In September the rookie returned to the Yankees. His first major league appearance was as a pinch hitter against Al Hollingsworth. He fanned on three pitches. But once the pennant was clinched, Huggins decided to begin resting some regulars. One would be Wally Pipp, the first baseman.

"You're starting at first today, Lou," said Hug in his quiet fashion. Gehrig rushed excitedly from the dugout as Bullet Joe Bush, the veteran pitcher, bore down on the Midget Manager in angry fashion.

"I don't want that clumsy clown playing first," growled Bush. "This game doesn't mean anything to you because you have the pennant clinched. But it means a lot to me. I've won nineteen this season and I get a bonus if I win twenty. I don't want that tanglefoot lousing up plays on me."

Huggins ignored him. Soon Gehrig made Bush look like a prophet. The slick Joe Judge bunted down the first base line. Lou lumbered in, scooped up the ball and froze as a runner scored from third. Bush started to spout sparks. By the eighth inning he was losing, 5 to 2, when the Yanks mounted a rally. They got two men on and Babe Ruth was the hitter. No sense in taking a chance on Ruth, particularly when the next batter was the green pea from Columbia, Gehrig. Ruth was walked to fill the bases. Then matters were made worse in a pressure-laden situation. Owen Bush, the Washington manager, yanked his starting pitcher and replaced him with Ray Francis, a left-hander.

Gehrig looked questioningly at Huggins. Green as he was, he still knew that smart managers don't ordinarily let inexperienced left-handed hitters face experienced left-handed pitchers in clutch situations. But Hug merely nodded in the direction of the bat rack. Lou selected his bat and Bush groaned out loud.

"I want to win this one, Hug," pleaded the pitcher. "Don't

let that kid bat. He still hasn't made his first hit in the majors."

"This can be very interesting," said Hug, more to himself than to Bush. Here was a test of nerve and of reaction under fire that might tell him a lot. Nor did the Midget Manager have long to wait.

Francis burned one in. Gehrig sent the ball rocketing to deep right. It crashed off the fence for a double and the score was tied as the speeding Ruth—he was fast in those days—winged all the way in from first, sliding under the throw to the plate. That three-run double evened the count at 5-all and the Yanks eventually won, 6 to 5.

It would be nice to write that a star was born that day. However, it would not be the truth. It took longer than one big hit. Gehrig had a total of twenty-six at bats that year and an average which was deceptively high at .423. He was worth further inspection at spring training in New Orleans the next season.

Gehrig reported with $10 in his wallet, a sum he had to stretch throughout the next six weeks. Legend has it that Lou was so broke that he took a job as a waiter. It's only a legend, though. The big kid was so desperate that he did toy with the idea. He and Benny Bengough, the young catcher, got as far as a restaurant door. But before they even opened it, they spotted Babe Ruth, Waite Hoyt and other Yankee free spenders, dining in regal fashion. They slunk away.

In those days the ballplayers didn't even receive pin money as they do today, a weekly payment of $25 for laundry, tips and incidentals. In 1924 they didn't get a dime until the season began. So Gehrig's working capital of $10 was near poverty.

One evening he was wandering around the streets of New Orleans. It was free and that's all he could afford. He encountered Dan Daniel, the baseball writer. The big fellow looked so sad that Dan spoke sharply to him.

"What's wrong with you?" he asked.

"I'm so broke, Dan," said Lou, "that I'll have to find myself a job somewhere."

"Nonsense," snorted Dan indignantly. "You're a member of the New York Yankees and they don't do things like that. Tell Huggins what the score is. He'll help you."

"I couldn't do that," said Lou.

If Gehrig couldn't, Daniel could. The writer explained the situation to Huggins, and the Midget Manager promptly gave Lou a big advance on his salary in order to tide him over.

Hard work never scared Gehrig. He came from industrious German stock. His mother was a domestic and his father was a handyman. As a boy Lou played baseball on the streets of the East Side and worked at whatever odd jobs he could find, dutifully bringing the pennies, nickels and dimes to the mother he absolutely adored. When his mother became cook at a Columbia fraternity house while his father tended the furnace, the pudgy kid idolized the varsity athletes and didn't even dare dream that he might become one himself.

He was a fat little boy with black curly hair. He got his first pair of long pants just before the High School of Commerce played Lane Tech at Wrigley Field in Chicago for the schoolboy championship. Lou was fifteen years old when he received instructions from his coach, Harry Kane, in the seventh inning of that game.

"Hit one out of the park," said Harry. It was a ridiculous assignment, a fifteen-year-old schoolboy hitting one out of a major league ball park. But Lou did it and won the game.

This, however, was a one-day sensation. Gehrig batted

less than .200 as a schoolboy and was a dreadful fielder. It was his football ability that brought him to Columbia. He didn't finish college because the Yankees offered him the magnificent bonus of $1,500 for signing and a salary of $3,000 a year. Lou grabbed at it because his father had to go to the hospital for an operation and there just wasn't any money in the family till.

The key date in the Gehrig story was June 1, 1925. In the eighth inning he pinch-hit for Pee Wee Wanninger, the shortstop, and the Iron Horse was on his way. He was not to miss a game for fourteen years, an unbelievable total of 2,130 consecutive games.

The next afternoon Wally Pipp, the regular Yankee first baseman, reported to Huggins as soon as he entered the clubhouse.

"I have a headache that's killing me, Hug," said Wally.

"That's all right, Wally," said Hug soothingly. "Take a couple of aspirins and I'll let you rest."

In later years Wally was able to laugh about it. "Some rest," he joshed. "I didn't get to play again until the following season and by then I was with a different team in a different league. I haven't been able to swallow an aspirin tablet since." Pipp wound up with Cincinnati in the National League. Gehrig had made it.

It wasn't easy, though. There was so much to learn.

"I used to mangle one play a game in the beginning," Lou ruefully recounted. "Then it was once a week and finally once a month."

He batted .295 in that first season but had twenty-one homers. Then it was .313 with sixteen homers in 1926. After that he roared up to .373 and forty-seven homers behind Ruth's epic sixty-homer year of 1927. Behind Ruth? Ah. That was the story of Gehrig's life. He spent a major part of it in the Babe's shadow.

He knew it, too. Maybe that's even the way he wanted it. They called him the Crown Prince and he didn't object. When the King of Swat departed, the suggestion was made to Lou by Tom Meany, the writer, that at long last Gehrig would get the headlines.

"No," said Lou with his simple directness. "I'm not a headline guy. I know that as long as I was following Ruth to the plate I could have stood on my head and no one would have known the difference. When the Babe was through at the dish, whether he hit one or fanned, nobody paid any attention to the next hitter. They all were talking about what the Babe had done."

Ruth's shadow? Escape was impossible. When the life-time averages of the two great teammates were finally compiled, the Babe produced an average of .342 to Gehrig's .340. It was only a mite behind the Babe, but behind him just the same.

Even the fates seemed to conspire against the Iron Horse. In 1931 the hulking Gehrig hit a screamer into the distant bleachers. It was struck with such violence that it caromed back into the glove of a Washington outfielder. Lyn Lary was the runner on first base with two out when the shot was hit. All he saw was the ball land in the outfielder's glove and he assumed the inning was over.

So he eased up as he neared third base and then jogged directly to the dugout. Gehrig, running with his head down —homer hitters usually don't have to take in the scenery —toured the bases. He was declared out for passing a base runner and his homer was reduced to a triple.

This became tremendously important at the end of the campaign. Ruth finished with forty-six homers. So did Gehrig. Thus did they tie for a home run championship that Lou actually won with his nullified forty-seventh. Not until 1934, when the Babe was washed up and at the end of his Yankee career, did the Iron Horse take a homer title. He did it with forty-nine, repeating with the identical figure in 1936. Oddly enough, those were the only home run crowns he ever won.

The Ruthian shadow that fell across Gehrig was always present and, strangely enough, Lou never resented it. The Babe was boisterous and showy. Whatever he did was like a 21-gun salute. Gehrig was a cap pistol, exploding decorously in a closet.

Take, for example, the Babe's extraordinary feat of calling the turn on the home run off Charlie Root in the 1932 World Series. The King of Clout ostentatiously pointed to the stands so that everyone would know what he promised to do. Then he did it.

As the beaming Babe crossed the plate, a grinning Gehrig clasped his hand in a fervent congratulatory handshake.

"It's your turn, kid," shouted the happy Babe. "You do the same thing."

"I will," promised Larruping Lou. He hit the first pitch for a home run. The entire world knew that Ruth had delivered on schedule. No one knew that Gehrig had performed the identical deed—but without showmanship.

And if it wasn't Ruth's shadow, it was someone else's shadow that kept obscuring him. On June 3, 1932, the Yankees played the Athletics in Philadelphia's Shibe Park. Gehrig hit three homers off George Earnshaw, the starting pitcher, and Connie Mack eventually replaced the big Moose with Lee Maheffey.

"Sit beside me, George," said Baseball's Oldest Inhabitant. "You've been pitching Gehrig wrong and I want you to watch how Mahaffey does it."

Gehrig hit the first pitch to the opposite field for his fourth homer.

"Now I understand, Mister Mack," said Earnshaw tartly. "Mahaffey made him change his direction."

It was four homers in a game and no one had done that since Ed Delahanty had achieved the feat thirty-six years earlier. What's more, it almost was five homers. Al Simmons made an incredible catch against the fence as Lou was rounding second base, thereby cutting off an inside-the-park homer that would have been an unprecedented fifth.

"Nice going, Lou," said a delighted Marse Joe McCarthy in the clubhouse afterward. "No one can take this day away from you."

Typically, someone did. Gehrig's feat was a front-page story in an era when only the most heroic of sports achievements hit the sacrosanct front pages of the newspapers. But this was the day when John McGraw resigned as manager of the New York Giants. The Yankee writers were just about to launch into long-winded rhapsodies about Gehrig when they received terse telegrams from their sports editors.

"Keep it short," they were advised. "McGraw just resigned."

So McGraw got the front page and column after column on the inside. Gehrig's homers were buried. There was never a complaint, of course. That just wasn't Lou's way.

The man seemed indestructible. He was an iron man even though they called him the Iron Horse. Once when he was running a high fever, the usually unsentimental Ed Barrow gazed out the window of the Yankee office and spotted a small cloud on the distant horizon. So he called off the game because of "threatening weather." Not a drop fell. But a day later Lou was ready for action.

The closest call, perhaps, came in July of 1934. Gehrig was felled by an attack of lumbago on the eve of a series with the league-leading Tigers in Detroit. The Bronx Bombers, knowing that the doctor had ordered Larrupin' Lou not to play, were warming up in dull, listless fashion when they suddenly came to life. Out of the dugout in uniform emerged the Iron Horse.

He hobbled out stiffly, encased in yards of adhesive tape in order to ease the pain. It didn't work. He got a base on balls in his first at bat and a single in his second. Then he could do no more. He had to quit.

The lumbago was worse the next day and the Yankees left Gehrig back in the hotel. But a few moments before game time a taxi pulled up at Briggs Stadium. His face creased with pain, Lou dragged himself out. He was in full uniform. He had dressed at the hotel.

This was a desperation move, however. Manager McCarthy knew that this could only be a token appearance. When he handed his lineup to the umpires, they blinked in astonishment. Listed as the Yankee lead-off hitter and formally designated as *shortstop* was Gehrig. The crippled hero promptly singled and retired, the regular shortstop, Frank Crosetti, replacing him as a base runner.

It had to be the end of that glorious endurance record. All the Yankees were sure of it. But the Iron Horse had an iron determination, a flaming will to win.

"I'll play tomorrow," he said through clenched lips. "I'll play the entire game, too."

He could not resist the challenge that was coming up. Schoolboy Rowe was to pitch that day and the Schoolboy was baseball's hottest pitcher. He was rolling inexorably with a 16-game winning streak.

Larrupin' Lou kept his promise. He played the entire game, constantly in pain and hobbled by the restrictive adhesive tape. Only a Gehrig could have done what he did. He slashed four hits off the supposedly invincible and untouchable Rowe, and three of them were ringing doubles off the wall.

Awed historians checked back at the completion of the three-game series and gasped. At a time when he should have been in the hospital, Gehrig hammered out six hits in seven at bats.

Lou was strong enough to fight off all ordinary ailments and injuries. It took the extraordinary to stop him. This came in such sneaky fashion that none was aware of its approach. Halfway through the 1938 season, Gehrig fell into a slump. Although his batting average dropped to .295 and his homer total to twenty-nine, there was no alarm. All ballplayers have "just one of those years" when everything goes wrong at once. Most snap back to normal the following campaign. But the reason for Gehrig's decline was far deeper.

In spring training of 1939 he seemed to have lost all his power at bat. His fielding, which hard work had made polished and slick, again degenerated into the clumsy tanglefoot style of his freshmen year. The season began and doubts increased with it. The Yankees started to stare at him strangely.

It was on May 2 in Detroit that Gehrig reached a decision. He walked into McCarthy's private cubicle in the clubhouse.

"Joe," he said, "I'm benching myself. Better start Babe Dahlgren at first. I'm not helping myself or the ball club."

Marse Joe, not ordinarily a sentimentalist, gulped hard and tears welled into his eyes.

"Okay, Lou, if you want it that way," he said. "But why not give it another try?"

"I can't, Joe," said Gehrig. "There was a routine play in the last game. Johnny Murphy fielded a dribbler that I started after. I had trouble getting back to the bag for the put-out although it should have been easy. Everyone patted me on the back and shouted, 'Nice play, Lou.' When they start to feel sorry for you . . ."

He left the sentence unfinished. McCarthy argued no more. Dahlgren played first base that day and the astounding record of 2,130 consecutive games had come to an end.

The Yankees sent Lou to the Mayo Clinic for observation and diagnosis. On June 20 the report was made public. He was gripped by a rare disease, amyotrophic lateral sclerosis. This disease is vaguely related to infantile paralysis and attacks the motor pathways and the cells of the central nervous system, a progressive paralysis of sorts. Two years later he was dead.

On July 4, 1939, the Yankees held a Lou Gehrig Appreciation Day at the Yankee Stadium. All the old-time Yankees were there. The Babe gave Lou a bear hug at home plate and wept unashamedly. It was an emotional afternoon and nothing was more touching than the few simple words the Larruper spoke. Said he:

"I may have been given a bad break but with all this I have a lot to live for. I consider myself the luckiest man on the face of the earth."

Lucky? He was rarely that on the field of play. But in the admiration and affection and esteem of those who knew him best, he was lucky indeed.

7

KING STANLEY

Stan (The Man) Musial

WARREN SPAHN, the ancient left-hander of the Milwaukee Braves, was standing behind the cage as the National League All-Stars were taking batting practice before the game in San Francisco in 1961. One particular hitter intrigued him.

"Listen, kid," said the droll Warren, "you'll never become a good hitter unless you change that funny-looking batting stance of yours."

The hitter was Stanley Frank Musial of the St. Louis Cardinals, and so acute is the Musial sense of humor that he practically fell out of the batting cage as he doubled up with laughter.

"Too late, pal," sang out the Man.

It was manifestly too late. This was Musial's twentieth All-Star game and he already was in the twilight of a glorious career, a forty-year-old man whose heart still was young and whose reflexes—surprisingly enough—also were young.

Many, many years earlier another great pitcher, Ted Lyons of the White Sox, supplied what was, perhaps, the most accurate description of the unorthodox Musial style at bat.

"When he stands at the plate," said Lyons, "he looks like a kid peeking around the corner to see if the cops are coming."

Peculiar technique to the contrary, though, Stan the Man

95

has established himself as one of baseball's greatest hitters. More important, possibly, he also has established himself as one of baseball's finest personalities. The ever-laughing Musial not only ranks as the most popular of all ballplayers but he also is the least pretentious. He never acts like the great star he was for twenty years. He's as friendly and approachable as a rookie trying to make good and please everyone.

Not only is Musial far above the average but the story of his life is far different from that of the run-of-the-mill ballplayer. Stan's has richly romantic overtones and almost would seem to have fictional facets to it.

He was born in Donora, Pennsylvania, not far from Pittsburgh's Forbes Field, and his boyhood dream was that he'd some day reach the big leagues, preferably as a member of the Pirates. But his father, Lukatz Musial, had different ideas. Having fled from Poland, he wanted his son to be the complete American, one with a college education.

So gifted a basketball player was young Stan in high school that he was swamped with offers of athletic scholarships to many colleges. But he also was so gifted a left-handed pitcher that major league scouts were on his trail when he was only sixteen years old. Most persistent was Andy French of the St. Louis Cardinals. He offered a contract. Lukatz Musial, yearning for a college education for his son, flatly refused.

So Stan burst into tears, blubbering like a baby. That did it. His father suddenly realized that he'd fled from Poland to escape dictatorship. Yet here he was, dictating himself. He reached for the pen and signed the contract for his under-age son. Stan Musial was a ballplayer.

But it wasn't quite as easy as it might seem. Stan was a failure before he was a success, so discouraged that he came perilously close to quitting at the ripe old age of nineteen.

Part-time minor league play during summer vacations while he was finishing high school prepared the way for his first full season in organized ball. This was at Daytona Beach under the wise managerial eyes of Dickie Kerr, the stouthearted little left-hander who pitched the White Sox to two victories in the fixed World Series of 1919. He won from the Cincinnati Reds in spite of the fact that infamous teammates were trying to throw away the victories.

Kerr made such a fine pitcher out of Stan that the boy became an 18-game winner for Daytona Beach. But one day, while playing the outfield, he tried for a shoestring catch and fell heavily on his left shoulder. He came up with a dead arm. What good, he thought, is a left-handed pitcher with a dead left arm? No good.

It was an awkward time for the kid to make such a discovery. His child bride was awaiting her first-born and Stan saw himself as a washed-up ballplayer before he'd even begun. He went to Kerr.

"Don't worry, Stan," said the fatherly Kerr. "Why don't you and your wife move into our house with us? That will save you a lot of worries. I still think you'll make the big leagues. I'll try to make an outfielder out of you."

Opportunities for showing his gratitude and appreciation to Dickie were nonexistent. But when a son was born, he was named Richard Kerr Musial. That was the best that Stan could do at that time. But he never forgot and the feeling he bore Kerr never diminished. In 1958 the wealthy Musial did something he'd long wanted to do. He bought a house in Houston, Texas, and gave it to his benefactor, Dickie Kerr.

Was there ever a gesture in baseball as magnificent as that? In a fashion typical of the man, Stan tried to keep it a secret. But this was too warm, too glowing and too wonderful a story to stay secret long. News leaked out and

Musial was exposed—to his vast embarrassment—as the marvelous person he is.

Stan was still listed as a pitcher in 1941 when Branch Rickey, the shrewd and all-knowing head of the Cardinals, came to training camp to inspect him. The Mahatma watched him at bat and exploded.

"By Judas Priest!" roared Rickey. "That man's not a pitcher. He's an outfielder."

So the Cards shipped him to Springfield, a Class C team, that had a short right field, the perfect spot for a weak-throwing outfielder. He burned up the league with .379 and was promoted to Rochester, then Double A, where he batted .326. He spent the last month that season with the Cards, hitting .426. Thus did he make the tremendous jump from Class C to the majors in one campaign.

One September evening he went for a walk with John Drebinger of *The New York Times*.

"Gosh, Drebbie," said the wistful twenty-year-old, "I just hope I can last up here for a couple of years."

It was to be more than twenty and on seven occasions he was to win the National League batting championship. During most of those earlier years Stan merely hit the ball where it was pitched and his home run output was insignificant, anywhere from a dozen to a high of nineteen in 1947.

"I'm just a singles hitter," he used to chirp in his cheerful fashion.

But as he grew older, stronger and more experienced, he began to add power to his line drives. He began to get distance as well. In 1948 he not only won the batting crown with .376 but had thirty-nine homers as well. A year later he faded to .338 and thirty-six homers. That's when he made the discovery. He told me about it the next spring at the training camp in St. Petersburg, Florida.

"I got real fatheaded last year," he said with a big grin. "I got to thinking about the fact that I had hit thirty-nine homers and had never once taken deliberate aim at the fences. So I asked myself a question. 'If you can make thirty-nine homers without trying for even one,' I said to myself, 'how many do you think you could make if you really went after them in earnest?' A stupid question deserves a stupid answer. I gave it, too.

"The next season I went homer-crazy. I was swinging for the seats every time I went to bat. Fortunately, I took stock of myself at the halfway mark. I'd hit about a dozen homers and was barely batting .300. It was a shock. Not only had I stopped hitting homers but I'd also stopped hitting singles. That's when I resolved that I'd never again make a deliberate try for a home run."

He stuck to his resolution. In the second half of that season he went only for singles. But he lifted his average to .338 and his homer output to thirty-six. He'd proved something to himself. Never again did he ever aim for the fences— Oops. Sorry. He did once. Recently he told about it.

In 1954 he was performing in a doubleheader against the Giants.

"I did shoot for the moon that day," he said sheepishly. He is so overwhelmingly honest that his face assumes a guilty look at even a minor admission. "It was in the doubleheader and I was merely minding my business by trying to hit the ball solidly. I had connected pretty good four times and each went for distance.

"After I hit my fourth homer, the announcer boomed out the news that I'd equaled a major league record of four homers in an afternoon. That's when I got the idea and decided that I'd try for a fifth homer.

"Now Hoyt Wilhelm was pitching for the Giants and I

never had hit him and his knuckleball particularly well.
He threw me a knuckler and—oh, boy!—that fifth homer
was the best shot of them all. Wow! What a belt!"

Stan's admiration was not for the fellow who hit the ball.
It was for the majestic flight of the ball itself, as impersonal
an admiration as if the little white pill had been self-
propelled. Stan the Man broke out in laughter.

"When I got home that night," he said in obvious delight,
"my son, Dickie, remarked, 'Gee, Dad, those pitchers must
have fed you a lot of fat ones today.' How do you like
that for hero worship?"

The flippant treatment which Richard Kerr Musial gave
his old man indicates that the entire household has absorbed
his down-to-earth naturalness and lack of pretense.

He is such a likable sort that even his children kid him.
So does every ballplayer he meets. And Stan kids back. In
contrast to most great stars he has no temperament; he is a
monument of good nature.

In one All-Star game in Milwaukee the lead-off hitter
for the National League in the twelfth inning was Stanley
Frank Musial. He stepped up to the plate, laughing as Yogi
Berra dragged himself into the catcher's box.

"What's the matter, Yog?" said the grinning Musial.

"My feet are killin' me," moaned Yogi.

"Relax, Yog," joshed Stan. "I'll get you out of here in
a hurry."

So Musial clouted the first pitch over the fence for a
home run that ended the game, and Yogi was able to soak
his feet earlier than expected.

When Stan was still a comparatively young ballplayer
and had swept past the 2,000 mark in base hits, one of the
St. Louis writers, Bob Broeg, kidded him about it—even
the writers feel free to kid Musial.

"Next stop for you, Banjo," said Broeg, "is three

thousand hits." The most derisive term one baseball man can apply to another is to call him a banjo hitter, meaning that he can only strike feeble little bloopers over the infield. But when applied to someone like Musial it becomes a term of affection.

Stan shook his head.

"That's an awful lot of hits," he said slowly. "It seems impossible and yet I once saw a man do it, Paul Waner. Funny thing is that Waner was my idol when I was a kid in Donora. Keep reminding me of it."

In May of 1958 the great man needed no more reminders. His hit total had mounted to 2,999 as the Cardinals moved into Chicago. Freddie Hutchinson, the Redbird manager, had enough sense of the dramatic to want the big one to come before the hometown folks in St. Louis the next day. So he decided to play the game without Musial, sending him to the bullpen where he could bask in the sun.

But Hutch also had enough sense of the importance of victory to prevent it being outweighed by his sense of the dramatic. The Cubs were leading, 3 to 1, and the Cards advanced a runner to second. Reluctantly, Hutch summoned Stan from the bullpen to serve as a pinch hitter. Moe Drabowsky bent in a curve.

Musial uncoiled and lashed a drive to the left-field corner. It didn't have enough carry to go into the stands for a homer but dropped in for a double that touched off the winning rally. The game was halted.

With big Hutch leading the way, the Cards poured from the dugout to shake the hand and pound the back of a man who had just joined the ultraexclusive Three Thousand Hit Club. The umpires retrieved the ball and gave it to Stan as a memento. A pinch runner replaced the hero and the din was deafening as the Man jogged to the dugout, grinning from ear to ear.

He paused en route, however, and kissed a pretty blonde in a front-row box.

"Do you know that lady, Stan?" asked one of the many photographers who were recording his triumph for posterity.

"I better," laughed Stan. "That's my wife."

At every stop the St. Louis-bound train made that evening thousands of fans gathered to cheer. It was like a Presidential special, and Stan had to make speeches from the back platform. The words that brought the biggest roars of delight came when he said:

"Hey, you kids, no school tomorrow."

Thousands more greeted the train on its arrival in St. Louis. Few men have been more idolized by fellow citizens than Musial or—and this is an even more difficult test— by the teammates who know him best.

The Cardinals gave him a plaque on a night in his honor and this is the way it read:

> To Stanley Frank Musial, an emblem of esteem from his teammates. An outstanding artist in his profession; the possessor of many baseball records; a gentleman in every sense of the word; adored and worshipped by countless thousands; the perfect answer to a manager's prayer; to this, we, the Cardinals, attest with our signatures.

Was there ever a finer tribute paid anyone?

Stan prefers to describe himself as "a lil' ol' singles hitter." But he also is among the leaders as a home run hitter, too— even if he did attain most of them by accident.

8

KING EDWIN

Edwin (Duke) Snider

THE quickest way to start an argument within metropolitan New York during the middle 1950s was for someone on a street corner, or at any get-together, to make a flat statement as to who was the best center fielder in town. Fistfights often erupted and it mattered not which man was identified as the No. 1 operative—Duke Snider of the Dodgers, Willie Mays the Giants or Mickey Mantle of the Yankees. Since they all were performing sensationally at the same time and in the same city, there was justification for the support of each.

The three ballplayers, of course, took no part in the controversy. They let their actions speak for them. But they had to be a bit intrigued by it. One day the Duke brought his four-year-old son, Kevin, to Ebbets Field and put on a show for him. He made spectacular catches and slashed out four hits, including two home runs.

The happy father knew that his little boy would have to be tremendously impressed. Otherwise he never would have dared ask him the question as they drove home together.

"Kevin," said the Duke, "who is the world's greatest ball-player?" There was pride in his eye and a lilt in his voice as he asked it.

"Pee Wee Reese," said Kevin. They drove the rest of the way in total silence.

At Ebbets Field the swift and powerful Edwin Donald

Snider was known as the Duke of Flatbush. Brooklynites alternately cheered him unrestrainedly and gave him the bird. That's where he achieved his peak performances, in Flatbush. During his last five seasons on the banks of the not-so-stately Gowanus River, the Duke ripped off successive home run totals of 42, 40, 42, 43 and 40. Then the Dodgers moved to Los Angeles—and into the Coliseum.

Most of the ex-Brooks had never seen their new playpen, a huge and lopsided field where the left-field fence crowds in on top of the shortstop and the right-field fence can be seen only with the use of high-powered binoculars. Before their first game they were being feted in a parade downtown. So the Giants, who ordinarily would have taken batting practice after the Dodgers, took it first. They at least had familiarized themselves with the peculiar contours of O'Malley's Alley before the Dodgers had even straggled out of the tunnel for their first sight of this monstrosity.

Willie Mays, bubbling with energy and mischief, could hardly wait for the ex-Brooks to put in appearance. He stationed himself by the tunnel and shrieked boisterously when he spotted Snider. He ran into the shadows, grabbed the Duke by the hand and led him forth.

"Look, Duke," he babbled in his shrill voice, one hand pointing toward the distant right-field fence. "They just took away your bat."

No one could have expressed it better. In effect, the Dodgers did take away the Duke's bat. His power zone had always been to right field and to center field and he had spent most of his career bombing passing automobiles in Bedford Avenue on the other side of the Ebbets Field wall. But in Los Angeles he was licked. In that first year in L. A. he hit one homer over the right-field fence, one over the left-field fence and only fifteen in all.

The Dodgers knew they had something special when they

signed the Duke as a seventeen-year-old Los Angeles school-boy in 1944. His bonus was an insignificant $750. But this 200-pound six-footer could run and throw and field and hit with power. He had all the ingredients.

But he also was moody and temperamental. Manager Jake Pitler of Newport News ordered the Duke to take a pitch without swinging at it. Young Snider couldn't resist. He swung and popped up. It cost him $25. At Montreal another take sign was given him by Clay Hopper, the manager. The Duke hit a home run, a rather expensive out because he was fined $50 for hitting it.

One day in Brooklyn he was flashed the bunt sign by Burt Shotton, his boss. Angrily, he obeyed. But when he popped up he also popped off and was spouting sparks when he returned to the dugout.

"Imagine asking a .320 hitter to bunt," he shouted.

"Imagine a .320 hitter popping up," snorted Shotton. Then he fined his hotheaded hired hand $25 for his impertinence.

But it was Shotton who really straightened him out. Snider is a left-handed hitter. Because the Dodger batting order of that era was overloaded with strong-muscled right-handed swingers—Snider was the only lefty—the Brooks faced an unending sequence of right-handed pitchers. Since the Duke rarely was called upon to face a southpaw, he generally was helpless at the plate when one took the mound against him.

The day came when Curt Simmons of the Phils, a left-hander, was due to pitch.

"I'd just as soon sit this one out, Burt," said the Duke.

"If you're going to sit on the bench," snarled the supposedly gentle and fatherly Shotton, "you won't sit on my bench. You can do it—back in Montreal."

Snider never did become effective against lefties but at

Duke Snider levels off in the batting cage. When the Dodgers played in Brooklyn, the Duke's booming bat broke up many a ball game.

least he stopped ducking them. He was on his way to become a polished ballplayer.

In the postwar year of 1947 the wise Branch Rickey had practically cornered the market on talented young athletes. One of them at the Cuidad Trujillo training camp was Snider. The ball went a mile when he hit it. But far too often he struck out. Rickey was appalled.

"Take that boy to Vero Beach," he ordered George Sisler, the expert on batting, "and teach him where the strike zone is located."

The Duke learned slowly but there were to be times throughout his career when folks couldn't help but wonder if he hadn't misplaced the location of that strike zone. In his first season as a full-fledged regular in 1949, he led the league in the one department where no one wants to lead— most strikeouts. The Duke had ninety-two.

A year later the handsome young Californian seemed to have arrived. He batted .321 and hammered out thirty-one homers. But he still swung too hard and one of his smashes was so beautifully tagged that it cost the Dodgers a pennant. This was ironic and also a bit freakish.

The Brooks and the Phillie Whiz Kids were locked in a titanic battle for the championship, a race that went down to the final game of the season when the two teams met at Ebbets Field. They went into the ninth with the score tied and the Dodgers had the fleet Cal Abrams on second base.

Although Abrams was fast, he was a bad base runner. No one should have known better than Milt Stock, the Brooklyn third base coach. Snider was the batter. He ripped a scorcher over second, a line drive so fierce that it skipped on one bounce into the glove of Richie Ashburn, the weakest-throwing outfielder in the league.

Abrams was off at the crack of the bat and Stock waved

him home. But he failed to take into consideration the fact that the Duke had blasted a ball with such velocity it was in Ashburn's glove on one big hop even before Abrams had made an unnecessarily wide turn at third. Richie was racing in with such momentum that, weak arm and all, he still threw out the runner at home by ten feet. The Phils won the game and the pennant on Dick Sisler's home run in the tenth.

So both the Duke and the Dodgers missed the World Series. They had been in it the year before—against the Yankees, naturally, and that's one Snider would prefer to forget. He batted .143 and struck out eight times to tie a record.

But he had a real wingding in 1952. He batted .345 and crashed out four homers. In fact the Duke's World Series marks touch both ends. He holds the National League record with ten homers and also with thirty-three strikeouts.

"He doesn't have to swing that hard," Joe DiMaggio once said. "The Duke has so much power that he still could belt the ball over the fence."

Perhaps the strangest season the Flatbush idol had was that 1952 campaign when he erupted in a real fireworks display in the post-season festivities. He was entitled to it, though; he had been red-hot all through the stretch.

In mid-August, however, the Duke was limping along with a .280 pace. Alarmed by the fact that the Giants were beginning to close in on him, Manager Charlie Dressen waited until the left-handed Curt Simmons was about to pitch against the Brooks and then he benched the Duke. The one fellow who interpreted this in sinister fashion was Mike Gaven, a baseball writer. He conferred with various sources, none of whom was identified, and wrote a carefully phrased story.

Dressen had permanently benched Snider, "baseball's greatest potential star," who would be given the maximum 25 percent salary cut that winter and probably traded.

When that story was printed, Snider blew his top. His handsome face grew beet red up to his prematurely gray hair. He confronted Gaven.

"I oughter punch you in the nose," he shouted. "Who told you that tripe you printed?"

"I'm not revealing my sources of information," said Mike loftily, refusing to back away from his statement.

Snider was so mad that he returned to the lineup and tore the league apart, batting close to .400 for the rest of the way. The Dodgers took the championship and gathered to celebrate Walter O'Malley's first victory party as Dodger president.

"Well, Mike," said O'Malley to Gaven, "I guess we have to give you credit for the pennant."

"How come?" said Mike who hadn't swung a bat or thrown a ball.

"Your story on Snider lit the fire that won for us," said O'Malley.

That also was the year when Snider had dinner one night in Chicago with a former teammate, Willie Ramsdell, then a pitcher with the Cubs. Like all ballplayers they chatted in uninhibited fashion.

"I can always get you with my knuckler," said Ramsdell.

"No, you can't," said Snider. "I can hit your knuckler. It's your slow curve that bothers me most."

The next afternoon Ramsdell was on the mound for the Cubs. His first pitch to the Duke was a slow curve. The Duke was indignant.

"Throw me that blankety-blank curve again," he bellowed, "and I'll knock it out of the park."

Ramsdell threw him the slow curve. Snider knocked it out of the park.

The Duke was primarily a streak hitter but Brooklyn fans seemed to love him anyway, even when he was in the depths of a slump. But Brooklynites are a breed apart. One afternoon in 1955 Snider had a dreadful session at bat. The Flatbush Faithful, unpredictable as ever, turned violently on him and booed him in merciless fashion. The Duke bristled and then exploded.

"These are the worst fans in the league," he snapped, virtually biting the hand that was feeding him. "They don't deserve a pennant."

His blast at the Ebbets Field populace was printed in every newspaper and curious baseball writers went to the park the next day to weigh the amount of venom in the fan reaction. They would really blister their fallen idol. Everyone was sure of that.

Cautiously the Duke stuck his head out of the dugout and there was a wild roar from the mob. Jeers? No, sir, they were cheers. The Brooklyn fans gave Snider an ovation. This so moved him that he got three hits and promptly was convinced that this was the best of all possible worlds and that Brooklyn was its capital.

Twice in his career the Duke slammed three homers in a game and twice he missed a fourth homer by no more than a foot.

"That's the story of my life," he said, holding his hands a foot apart. "I'm this far from the top."

It was an accurate analysis. He has come so close to being a Hall of Fame candidate but will never make it in spite of his enormous talent. Somehow or other he has been just a trifle short of going over the top.

9

KING MICKEY

Mickey Charles Mantle

THE first major league ball park that Mickey Mantle ever saw was Ebbets Field in Brooklyn. The exhibition series for the 1951 spring training program was approaching a conclusion and Master Mickey, a bewildered boy of nineteen, had found himself swept along in a current that was moving much too fast for him.

A few months earlier he had been playing shortstop for Joplin in a Class C league, and now he was about to take his place in the Yankee outfield alongside the great Joe DiMaggio. No wonder his mind was in a whirl. What's more, the hard-boiled baseball writers had been extravagant in their praise of his training camp showing.

Even Casey Stengel got into the act. Said he: "This is a kid which is gonna be tree-menjous." He naturally used the Stengelese pronunciation of tremendous.

Shortly before the Yankee-Dodger exhibition began, Ol' Case took his infant prodigy on a personally escorted sightseeing tour of Ebbets Field. Finally they paused in front of the fence that jutted out at all sorts of odd angles.

"This is a fence which the ball bounces off kinda funny-like," he began.

"Uh huh," said Mantle.

"I oughter know," said Stengel proudly. "After all, I wuz the right fielder on the Brooklyn ball club for six seasons."

"You were?" said Mantle, incredulity in his voice.

The Ol' Perfessor started to laugh. He chuckled all the way back to the dugout where a covey of newspapermen awaited him.

"This kid is so green," cackled Ol' Case, jerking a thumb in the direction of Master Mickey, "that I'm sure he thinks I started my major league career at the age of sixty as manager of the Yankees."

Mantle was to learn better, of course. He was to learn a lot of things. Yet he never quite became the monument of enduring and consistent greatness that Stengel hoped to leave behind him. There was one glorious season when Mickey was truly "tree-menjous." That was in 1956 when he won the rare prize of the Triple Crown, leading the league in batting with .353, in homers with fifty-two and in runs-batted-in with 130. He also swept the Most Valuable Player distinction that season.

He repeated as MVP in 1957 when he attained a mark of .365, his top average, and Stengel's bright dreams of a permanent mantle of greatness for Mantle never shone brighter. Yet the Oklahoma Kid failed to achieve the consistency that marked the careers of the super stars.

He was to slough off until he dipped under .300, the dividing line between the fair hitters and the genuinely good ones. The strange part about Master Mickey, however, is that he'd still be the most feared batsman on the Yankees even if he were hitting .086. His power is awesome and the Switcher can belt a ball a mile from either side of the plate, although he is frank to admit, "I can hit further right-handed." Why, then, didn't he just concentrate on swinging from that one side?

"I'd bat right-handed all the time," he said with a sly grin, "if the right-handed pitchers would promise not to throw curves."

Mantle was one problem Stengel never fully solved or

could explain during their decade together on the Yankees. The wily Ol' Perfessor had plenty of company in his bafflement, though. Those expert analysts, the baseball writers, haven't solved him, either.

Master Mickey presumably has all the physical equipment. He has the back muscles of a professional strong man; he is powerfully built. Yet he still is one of the fastest men afoot in the majors. He fields expertly and has a fine arm. He has studied his trade well.

It isn't that he's lazy or lacks pride. He's an industrious workman and his pride is so fierce that it lashes him into playing when common sense would dictate that he rest whatever injuries or ailments he has at that particular moment.

The Oklahoma Kid damaged his left leg during a high school football game and osteomyelitis, a bone infection, resulted. Three times he was turned down by the draft board and on the fourth occasion his case was meticulously reviewed by the Surgeon General. He again was turned down.

The mere fact that exhaustive Army tests found him unfit is in itself proof positive of the seriousness of his ailment. Furthermore a chronic knee defect followed his stepping into a drainage hole in the Yankee Stadium outfield during his first World Series in 1951. He went down as if shot. The knee has bothered him, on and off, ever since. Far more often than the average ballplayer, Mantle has come up with injuries—sprains, bruises, muscle tears, viruses, allergies, colds and assorted other medical mishaps.

When the M-Boys, Mantle and Maris, took dead aim at Babe Ruth's record of sixty homers in the exciting 1961 series, Master Mickey came down with a virus in the September homestretch. The sparkle went out of him. He grew wan and listless. Three weeks before the end of the 154-game span, the big blond surrendered.

"I can't make it," he said dispiritedly. "I couldn't even make it within the full 162 games."

He practically stopped hitting homers. At 154 games he had fifty-three. He added one later during the extra eight games of the expanded schedule, but by the final few days of the season he was in the hospital. The infection had settled in his right hip and an abcess had to be lanced, knocking him out of the start of the World Series. This marked the fourth time in nine post-season classics that Master Mickey had been forced into the role of a part-time performer.

The onetime Boy Wonder was in the hospital when the regular campaign came to an end. He was watching that last game on television in the hope that his roomie, Maris, would belt his sixty-first homer. (He did, too.) A man in Seattle had offered $5,000 to the fan who caught the ball and returned it. That fact was constantly being repeated by the television announcers.

Suddenly the telephone in the Yankee clubhouse rang. Pete Sheehy, the custodian of the dressing quarters, answered.

"This is Mickey Mantle," said the voice.

"Oh, yeah?" said Pete suspiciously. Then came the instant recognition. It really was Mantle. "Hiya, Mick," said Pete.

"I want an announcement made over the public address system," said Mantle from his hospital bed. "Tell the fans that Mickey Mantle will pay $5,000 to anyone who catches a home run ball hit by Whitey Ford. Got it, Pete? Hey, wait a minute. Maybe you'd better make it a hundred bucks. That lucky stiff might accidentally hit one."

Pete laughed and promptly ignored the request. But he marveled at the way Mantle had developed and matured. Here he was, making with the jokes despite his pain, a man of poise and a sense of humor. Pete had seen Yankees come and go since Babe Ruth's day. He could remember them all. And he also could remember the nineteen-year-old Mantle when he first reported to the Bronx Bombers—a shy, bewildered, awkward, and scared hayseed who was totally awed by the big city and the big city's winningest ball club.

Mantle came from Commerce in the northeast corner of Oklahoma. From the time he was born his father, a frustrated ballplayer named Elvin C. Mantle, had directed the boy's destinies toward the big leagues. The start came right at the beginning, at the christening.

The blond, blue-eyed boy was not named Michael. He was named Mickey in honor of his Old Man's idol, Mickey Cochrane. Ironically enough, Cochrane's true monicker is Gordon. But no matter. By the time the kid was six years old his father was pitching left-handed to him, and his grandfather, Charles Mantle, was pitching right-handed to him. He was a switch hitter before he had the slightest comprehension of what baseball was or meant. By the time he was ten he was in a Pee Wee League and soon was so good that he was able to handle himself in competition with boys far older than he.

In 1948 Tom Greenwade, one of the shrewdest and most perceptive of all the Yankee scouts, was on the prowl for talent in Joplin, Missouri. With him was Kenny Magness, a friend who was a fireman in Joplin.

"While you're down this way, Tom," said Magness, "you ought to take a look at a kid in Commerce. He's not very big but he looks like a natural hitter. He's only sixteen and should grow. They call him Little Mickey Mantle."

Greenwade jotted down the name. He took a look. His eyes popped.

"I caught up with him later that summer," said Tom. "He didn't even know I was there. I saw him hit one over the fence left-handed and another over the other fence right-handed. But when I saw him run—wow! That's when I knew. I did some running myself to find out when his high school class graduated so that I could grab him."

When the deadline of graduation day arrived, Greenwade made the grab. The price was ridiculously low, $1,500. And that included $140 a month for the remainder of the season with a Class D team as a shortstop. A year later Mickey was a shortstop for Joplin. Then came a bid to the instructional (Stengel always pronounced it "instructural") school that the Yankees ran before the start of spring training. Mantle was an instant sensation, so good that he was leaped all the way to the varsity. It was a shattering experience for a greenhorn from the sticks.

"I don't think I ever could forget opening day of 1951," he once told me, shuddering at the memory. "It was the worst day of my life. I don't think I slept a wink the night before and I was trembling all over from the moment I reached the Yankee Stadium.

"To tell you the truth, I don't remember much about that game. It was a blur to me. I think I grounded out to third in my first at bat and I know I drove in a run. I take no credit for it. I was so scared I just shut my eyes and swung. I didn't see a pitch all day. I was too scared."

Mantle batted well over .300 from the start. But the pitchers' union has a grapevine which is the world's fastest communication system. The word quickly got around— pitch the kid outside when he bats righty and inside lefty. His strikeouts soon outnumbered his hits, and in mid-July he was farmed out to Kansas City, then in the Triple A American Association. A month later he was back for keeps, the minor league interlude being so brief that many fans are still unaware of the fact that it ever happened.

At the start of the 1953 season, however, something happened which may have greatly retarded the Mantle development as a super star. He hit a home run. But what a home run it was!

This was his famous "tape-measure" effort in Washington. He hit one over the deep center-field bleachers and out of the ball park. The enterprising Red Patterson, the Yankee publicist, whipped out his trusty tape measure as soon as a small boy pointed out where the Mantle blast had come to earth. The distance was 565 feet, hitherto unattainable by anyone except Babe Ruth.

Master Mickey's thinking was warped by the magnitude of that shot. He swung so violently that his strikeout totals zoomed up alarmingly, much to the consternation of Stengel. Yet such was Casey's pride in his protégé that he often compounded the difficulties by boasting about Mantle's distance achievements. He began babbling to me one day at the Yankee Stadium.

"A tree-menjous ballplayer," began Ol' Case, never bothering to identify Mantle by name. "Don't matter what ball park he's in. See that last exit in the upper deck in left field. Look. Way up there almost over the bullpen. His hit was still climbin' when it landed which scattered seats all over somethin' terrible. But if the stands didn't get in the way the ball would have gone outta the stadium. Or you take the Pittsburgh park, which nobody hit a ball outta until Ruth did it and so did Mantle which don't get many opportunities to hit there on account of his age."

That last sentence didn't add up properly. But no matter.

"One of those homers Mantle hit in Washington woulda been travelin' yet except it strikes a tree outside the park. They tell me that the only other feller which hit that tree was Ruth. He shook some kids outta the tree when the ball landed. But the tree's gotten bigger in the last twenty-five years and so, I guess, have the kids which the Babe shook outta it. All he's gotta do is cut down his strikeouts." Casey meant Mantle, not Ruth.

In his early years Master Mickey would get so mad at striking out that he'd storm red-necked back to the dugout and vent his spleen on the water cooler by kicking it savagely. The other Yankees prankishly wrapped up the water cooler in a big cardboard box labeled MANTLE'S KICKING POST. Master Mickey didn't think it at all funny.

He would now, though. Billy Martin drew him out of his shell and, when Martin was traded, the Oklahoma Kid took to consorting with the witty Whitey Ford, who sharpened his sense of humor and taught him to laugh.

Greatness is still awaiting Mantle; his potentialities are enormous. Mickey's story is still unfinished. The brightest chapters could very well lie ahead.

10

KING EDWIN II

Eddie Mathews

WHENEVER a major league ballplayer gets to meet the Commissioner, certain formalities are involved. The athlete nods respectfully, the Commissioner gives him a warm greeting and they shake hands. But Eddie Mathews did not follow protocol the first time he encountered Ford Frick. The third baseman of the Braves knocked down the sport's top executive.

This procedure is not normally recommended for young ballplayers—or even old ones. But in this instance it was strictly an accident. Frick was visiting the Braves' spring training camp at Bradenton in March of 1952 and he was wandering across the outfield during batting practice in the company of two writers.

Shagging flies at the time was a strong young bull named Edwin Lee Mathews, a twenty-year-old rookie. The man in the batting cage tagged one. The ball sailed out, far and deep. Eddie tore back after the ball in intense, single-minded pursuit. Big as he is—six feet two and 210 pounds—he also is surprisingly fast.

Unaware of approaching disaster, Frick and the two writers paused in a tight cluster as Mathews bore down on them like a runaway boxcar. Into the threesome he crashed and sprayed them over the landscape. Fortunately, no one was hurt. But of all the ballplayers he's met over the years Frick best remembers his introduction to Eddie Mathews.

Before this young man has completed his career, however, it is likely that he will be remembered by a lot of
people besides Frick, especially the historians. At his current rate of home run progress it would seem that he eventually will replace Mel Ott as the all-time National League
leader. Babe Ruth, of course, is out of reach but Mathews
might not find any of the immediate trailers beyond his
range.

Before Mathews brought himself to public attention as a
result of his forceful introduction to Frick, the Braves knew
they had someone special. They'd suspected as much when
they won him away from the fifteen other major league
clubs after his graduation from a Santa Barbara high school
in 1949. The rules said that all schoolboys were not to be
approached until after midnight of graduation day.

Fifteen scouts sat in a hotel lobby, waiting for the senior
prom to end. But in a hotel room Johnny Moore, the Braves
scout, was waiting with pen poised for the clock to reach
12:01. Waiting at his side was the seventeen-year-old Eddie
and his dad. They signed for $5,999 in order to duck under
the bonus rule.

Eddie was sent to High Point, a Class D team in the Caro-
lina State League, where he batted .363 and had seventeen
homers in only forty-three games. If any doubt as to his
potentiality still remained, it was dispelled when Lou Perini,
the owner of the Braves, was sounded out for a trade by
Branch Rickey, the Deacon of the Dodgers. Names were
discussed and agreement approached.

"It's a deal," snorted the Mahatma, fumbling through
some papers, "if you'll throw in some Class D player like
. . . harumph . . . what is that boy's name? . . . oh, yes,
Mathews."

It was all an act. Rickey knew everything about every
ballplayer in the land and he never had to fumble for names.

"No, thanks," said the perceptive Perini. "You're the best judge of talent in the business. If a kid on a Class D team interests you, he has to interest me even more."

Eddie served three years' apprenticeship in the minors and he wasn't even on the Braves' roster—they then were the Boston Braves—that spring in Bradenton. Paul Waner, once a great batsman and always an expert on hitting techniques, was assigned to study his style.

"There's nothing I can teach that boy about swinging a bat," said Big Poison. "He's perfect."

So they brought the boy to Boston and installed him at third base, making room for him by trading Bob Elliott to the Giants. Then happened something which was to warp Eddie's thinking for many years to come, perhaps even delay his rise to stardom.

He was only twenty when he played his first big league game, a darkly handsome boy with curly black hair and a flashing smile. But he didn't smile much. Naturally shy, he withdrew into his shell at training camp. He spoke little to anyone and not at all to the newspapermen. He gave yes and no answers reluctantly. So he was labeled surly and uncooperative. Even on the field he did not shout and holler or ham it up. So he also was labeled colorless.

Elliott had been popular with the press and his being traded brought some resentment. One typewriter pounder broke into print with sharp words.

The Braves traded a man who batted in more than 100 runs for a mere babe who looks as though he should be back in the baseball nursery.

So Mathews sulked and brooded as he began his feud with all sportswriters, a feud no athlete ever can win because the writer always has the last word. Yet the youngster did

Ed Mathews' slugging helped the Braves win two pennants. Before he retires he's sure to be in the top five all-time home run kings.

hit twenty-five homers in his freshman year. He got little acclaim for it.

The Braves were being driven out of Boston by gross neglect. The fans stayed away and only baseball writers, telegraph operators, ushers and park employees bothered to attend ball games. Eddie could walk the streets or go to restaurants and movies unrecognized. He got to like and treasure that privacy.

Then came the sudden switch to Milwaukee and everything was different. Every day was Christmas. Wild-eyed fans reacted like kids with new toys. They showered gifts on the players. They gave them no peace. They couldn't move a step without autograph hounds dogging them.

They soon felt like shady characters under constant surveillance. If a ballplayer stopped for a glass of beer, exaggeration twisted that into a condition of blind drunkenness. If he said hello to a girl, it became a torrid romance.

Fighting grimly for a privacy he no longer got, Eddie made things worse by clouting forty-seven home runs and hitting .302. He was the biggest hero of all. He was mobbed and bedeviled. Because he was so newsworthy, the writers and photographers pursued him in the line of duty. He resented them even though his adoring public clamored for stories and pictures about him.

The biggest publicity splash he got was one he didn't want. Being a handsome young bachelor, he grasped every opportunity to get away from it all. One day Bob Buhl, the pitcher who is his roomie on road trips, invited him to his home for dinner. Buhl lives on the far side of Milwaukee. It was a pleasant evening, so pleasant that time flew. Suddenly it was 2 A.M.

Mathews headed for his hotel in the heart of town. He drove fast because he was out after curfew. A police car pursued him and Eddie did a foolish, unthinking thing. He turned into a side street and turned off his lights in an effort to escape. The police car pulled alongside and the gendarmes recognized him instantly.

"You're Eddie Mathews, aren't you?" said the cop.

"Yes," said Eddie.

"Eddie," said the cop, "you've just done about as silly a thing as any man can do." He wrote out the summons.

Mathews appeared in court. So did writers and photographers. A cameraman aimed his trusty picture box.

"You take a picture of me," shouted Eddie, "and I'll break your neck."

"Not in my court," said the judge.

Eddie was fined $50 for reckless driving, the photographer got his picture, and Manager Charlie Grimm slapped on an extra $100 for violating curfew rules. It was a big story in Milwaukee.

It also was a big story in Milwaukee when the city's most eligible bachelor married a pretty Wisconsin girl, Virjean Lauby. Journalists and photographers showed up.

"If this wasn't my wedding day, buddy," said the groom to a lensman, "I'd break your neck."

However, marriage calmed down the hotheaded slugger. He learned to face life, not as he wanted it but as it was. Poise and maturity settled over him. While he never could become a darling of the press box like Yogi Berra, his public relations improved. He learned to spar with the press.

Once he had been so bad a fielder that he was referred to in print as a "butcher." But he worked tirelessly at his fielding, practicing hour after hour, until he became a good glove man.

In the 1957 World Series the change in him was obvious. In the beginning he couldn't hit at all but he fielded like a fiend. Reporters gathered at his locker after the second game.

"What are you in there for, Eddie—your glove?" asked a writer.

A few years earlier none would have dared ask that question. But this was the new Mathews.

"I guess so," he said, flashing his biggest smile and charming everyone within range. He discoursed for a while on his fielding and how hard he'd worked on it.

"How about your hitting, Eddie?" asked someone else.

"It isn't there," said Eddie pleasantly.

"Will it be tomorrow?" was the next question, a loaded one.

"Maybe," said Eddie. "My swing is good and my timing is good. The hits just aren't dropping."

The first one dropped when he doubled in the fourth game. But the big one dropped in the tenth inning when he arched a mighty drive over the right-field fence with a man aboard to end it with a 7–5 Milwaukee victory. The hits came more steadily thereafter, including his all-important "leg hit," a dribbler he outraced to drive in the lone run in the 1–0 fifth game.

It wasn't Eddie's bat but his glove that saved the seventh game and won the World Series for Milwaukee. The Yankees had filled the bases with two out in the ninth when Moose Skowron blasted a projectile down the third base line. With a graceful swoop that hardly is expected in one so big, Mathews backhanded the ball near the bag in a sensational stab. He leaped for the base in a force play to end the inning and then continued his wild dance of joy down the base lines. The Braves had upset the Yankees and won the World Series.

One of the unusual aspects of Mathews' hitting is that he never has had particular trouble with left-handed pitchers, although left-handed swingers ordinarily are in difficulty until they learn the knack. Eddie learned early.

"When I was with High Point," he once explained, "we had seven lefty hitters in the lineup. So other teams saved their lefties for us. Three out of five starters were lefty. And it almost was as bad when I joined the Braves. We had five lefty hitters. You learn fast that way."

His first major league home run, by the way, was off the left-handed Ken Heintzelman of the Phils, a 400-footer that landed on the street outside the Shibe Park fence in left center.

The high, inside pitch was once his weakness. News travels fast along the grapevine which seems to connect all pitchers to the same listening post. They fanned him so often on this one and he saw it so often that he finally learned to belt the high, inside pitch out of the ball park.

Public relations were once his weakness. He learned to handle that eventually but it took him a great deal longer than it did to overcome his baseball flaws. With his looks and personality he can become the charm boy of the major leagues.

The surest bet of all, though, is that Eddie Mathews will some day be the kingpin home run slugger of the National League.

11

KING RALPH

Ralph Kiner

IF Babe Ruth altered the course of baseball history by what he did, Ralph Kiner altered it by something he said. It isn't often that words can carry such impact, but a flippant observation which Kiner tossed over his shoulder one day influenced the thinking of an entire generation of ballplayers. Said he:

"Hitters who slice singles to the opposite field ride around in jalopies. The hitters who pull the ball into the stands for homers ride around in Cadillacs."

Perhaps Kiner was trying to explain why he was able to draw down a salary of some $90,000 a year, although he wasn't much of a batsman insofar as averages were concerned. If he didn't hit it often, however, he sure hit it far. Twice he threatened the Babe's record of sixty as he reached fifty-one homers in 1947 and fifty-four two years later.

But the message he delivered about the monetary value of the home run ball was engraved in the minds of all the ballplayers. Few nowadays choke up their grips on the bats and try to poke hits "where they ain't" in the Wee Willie Keeler tradition. They hold their bats on the end and swing for the fences.

Kiner was a strapping Californian, a solidly muscled 190-pounder who was not unlike Roger Maris in physique. He was a handsome man with a vast amount of charm and personality. But on the playing field he was colorless and only when he had a bat in his hands at the plate did he generate sparks and excitement.

He drew more than a million people to games of the bedraggled Pittsburgh Pirates and was so much the center of attention that fans normally filed quickly from the stands as soon as he took his last turn at bat. The game didn't interest them, only Kiner.

Ralph was a highly intelligent young man who was realistic enough to be aware of his limitations. He knew he had none of the flamboyance of a Babe Ruth, none of the gracefulness of a Joe DiMaggio and none of the all-around skill of a Willie Mays. As an outfielder he was slow-footed and barely adequate. But he also knew that the home run was his most important stock in trade and he was realistic in that, too.

When he began to crowd the Babe home run record in his most productive or fifty-plus seasons, he was deluged with mail, some 200 to 300 letters a week. Most of them blistered him for having the gall to threaten one of the most sacred of all baseball marks.

"I hope you never make it," snarled one typical missive. "You're not worthy to replace Ruth."

Perhaps Kiner agreed in his secret heart because he once wrote a magazine article, "The Home Run I'd Hate to Hit." It would have been the homer that erased from the books the Bambino's precious mark of sixty. However, he didn't get close enough to know whether he really would have hated it or not.

Ralph was always a slugger. Even as a schoolboy in Alhambra High, he clouted ten homers in a 24-game season. The Pirates grabbed him and sent him to the minors where he impressed no one. The war interrupted his baseball and he reported to the Pittsburgh spring training camp in 1946 before accepting the assignment destined for him with Hollywood in the Pacific Coast League.

The Pirate manager was Frank Frisch, the old Fordham Flash. He gave the rookie a whirl in batting practice and Kiner made his eyes bulge with his distance clouting. So the Flash started the big kid against the wily Bill Dietrich of the White Sox in an exhibition game at Pasadena. Kiner hit two homers over the center-field fence, more than 400 feet away.

"Ye gods!" shrieked Jimmie Dykes, the White Sox manager, who couldn't believe his eyes. "Where did you ever find him?"

"Never mind where I found him," said the dazed Frisch, "I just don't want to lose him."

Therefore, the Flash abandoned all plans of farming Kiner to the minors for another year and made him a regular. After six weeks he was starting to regret the move because Ralph was barely batting .100 and was failing to reach the fences. Suddenly the big Californian came to life and wound up with twenty-three homers. Obviously it was a subpar year in that department because Kiner found himself the home run champion, a title he was to own or share for seven years.

What settled Kiner into the proper groove was a move the Pirates made in 1947. They signed the aging Hank Greenberg, then near the end of an illustrious career. What's more, they made roommates of the old slugger and the young slugger. It was the start of a lasting and valuable friendship. The depth of that friendship was proven when Ralph married Nancy Chaffee, the tennis internationalist, in 1951. His best man was Greenberg.

Hammering Henry was the fellow who gave Kiner shortcuts and advice as they talked baseball night after night.

"I was able to capitalize on Hank's experience," Ralph

once explained, "and borrow from him things it might have
taken me years to discover by myself."

In spite of Greenberg, however, Kiner started poorly in
1947 and folks were saying that the sophomore jinx had
handcuffed him. But Hank kept striving to keep his new
buddy from losing confidence.

"Set your season's mark at twenty-five," he kept urging.

After a while he raised the sights. "Make it thirty," he
said.

Soon he shut up. Ralph needed no more artificial
boosters. He was off and winging, a hot hitter.

He was hottest in September and nowhere was he hotter
than one day in Chicago. He was so hot that he had a
temperature of 103, so riddled by flu bugs that he lay under
a pile of blankets on the trainer's table in the clubhouse
and shivered. He was unaware of the fact that the Pirates
were locked in a grossly untidy game with the Cubs. They
were being beaten, 12 to 9, when they got a runner on base.
Billy Meyer, the Pittsburgh manager, sent the batboy into
the clubhouse. He raced over to the feverish Kiner.

"Mr. Meyer wants to know," he said, "if you can get
into uniform and take one swing as a pinch hitter."

"I'll try," croaked the weakened Kiner, wiping the sweat
from his brow and pushing the blankets aside. He dressed
as quickly as he could. But by the time he had reached the
dugout, the Pirates had filled the bases.

"Go to it, boy," said Meyer, patting him on the back.

This sounds like one of those wildly fictional episodes
that's been yanked from the pages of Frank Merriwell or
dreamed up by a Hollywood scriptwriter.

Kiner took one swing. He hit a grand-slam homer that
won the ball game. Then he went to bed.

Even without a fever, though, he was hot that September.
On September 10 he bashed out two homers off Larry

Jansen of the Giants. A day later in a doubleheader with the Braves he got four more, off three different pitchers. A day later he crashed two of Red Barrett's offerings over the fence for an unprecedented crop of eight in four games.

At Ebbets Field that month Kiner hit the one which was to be his biggest thrill in baseball. It was his fiftieth home run.

"Nothing ever could match that," he said afterward with a satisfied grin. "It was a bigger kick than any I've ever had in baseball and probably will stay my biggest thrill until I hit sixty—if I ever do. I even forgot about my chance of tying the Babe. You see, number fifty meant something special to me. It meant that I'd arrived in a very exclusive club. Outside of the Big Fellow only Hank Greenberg, Jimmy Foxx, Hack Wilson and Johnny Mize have made it."

Kiner's pride was justified. The Fifty Homer Club is still a most exclusive one. During the intervening years only three new members have qualified, Willie Mays, Mickey Mantle and Roger Maris.

Although Ralph was popular to the point of idolatry with the Pittsburgh fans and the only gate attraction the Pirates had, his days became numbered when Branch Rickey assumed the front office control of the Buccaneers. One of the secrets of the Mahatma's success during his long years with the Cardinals and the Dodgers was his uncanny perceptiveness with players.

He never waited until an athlete was near the end of his string before trading him away. The deals were swung a year or two earlier in order to get a maximum return. As much as Rickey admired Ralph's big bat, crowd appeal and engaging personality, there were items about him that bothered the Mahatma.

The Kiner salary was $90,000 per annum. He was thirty years old and his slowness afoot was becoming accentuated.

Furthermore, the Top Branch envisioned a housecleaning that would replace the worn-out Pirates with young, eager whizbangs like the famous Gas House Gang he had used for revitalizing the Cardinals. So he peddled Kiner to the Chicago Cubs. Two seasons there and a final fling in the other league with one campaign with the Cleveland Indians finished out the Kiner career. It all added up to ten seasons in the big leagues. For Kiner it was a remarkable decade. Few men ever parlayed one extraordinary talent farther. In ten years he hit 369 home runs, an average of almost thirty-seven a season. During that time he was paid more than a half million dollars; $520,000 to be exact.

Because he could belt a baseball over fences, he didn't have to ride around in a jalopy. His slugging ability put him behind the wheel of a Cadillac, an item that was noticed by an entire generation of ballplayers.

12

KING JOSEPH

Joe Di Maggio

JOSEPH PAUL DiMAGGIO ended his baseball career when he was fourteen years old—or so he thought. Fortunately, he didn't make it stick. He just got bored with the kid team he played on in his native San Francisco. But a couple of years later he changed his mind when his big brother, Vince, became a minor-leaguer.

"If Vince can make dough playing ball," said Joe to himself, "I should do pretty good, too, because I can play better than he can."

For a fellow whose modesty was painful in his later years that statement was almost out of character. Perhaps it was only the brash confidence of extreme youth. But it spurred Joe into returning to the diamond with sandlot teams as— brace yourself for this—a third baseman and shortstop.

In 1932 Vince had been promoted to the San Francisco Seals of the Pacific Coast League and the Seals were bogged down in sixth place as the final few days of the season arrived. Augie Galan, the shortstop, asked for permission to leave the team with three games still to go.

"But who'll play shortstop for us?" asked the manager.

Vince spoke up quickly.

"I have a kid brother who can do the job for you," he said.

"Okay," said the manager. "Bring him around."

And that's how Joe DiMaggio, an outfielder of unsur-

passed skills, began his formal professional career as a shortstop. He was seventeen years old and scared to death. He was afraid to let go with the first ball he fielded and he lobbed the ball to first, barely nailing the runner.

"Throw the ball, you dumb busher," snarled Jules Wera, the veteran third baseman who had performed briefly with the Yankees.

On the next play Joe followed orders. He threw the ball with all the power of that strong right arm. It landed in the seventeenth row of the grandstand.

Despite such inauspicious beginnings Joe had earned a further trial with the Seals at spring training. By then his talent was unmistakable. He became an outfielder and soon found himself slightly embarrassed. The Seals traded off Vince and Joe was given his big brother's job. All he did in that freshman season was to bat .340. In the course of it he hit safely in sixty-one consecutive games, a forerunner of what was to come.

Big league scouts swarmed in on him, but Charlie Graham, the owner of the Seals, thought that delay would add sweetness to the honey. He could profit at the gate by having DiMadge on his ball club and then could sell him for an even higher price. It was a sound idea. But Graham didn't know about the DiMaggio jinx. It was starting to work.

Hardly had the 1934 season opened when Joe stepped out of a taxicab, something that's neither difficult nor dangerous. But in some peculiar fashion, his left knee popped on him and Joe had to spend six weeks in a splint. The big league scouts, who had been eager to grab him at any price, backed away. Only Bill Essick and Joe Devine of the Yankees were willing to gamble on buying him. So was George Weiss, then the head of the Yankee farm system. But Ed Barrow, the big boss, flatly refused.

"We've spent too much money on the farm system," growled Big Ed. "I refuse to buy ballplayers. From now on we'll develop our own."

So convinced were Messrs. Weiss, Essick and Devine of the DiMaggio potential that they did something no one ever had dared do before. They went over Barrow's head. They drove to French Lick Springs and put the proposition before Colonel Jacob Ruppert, the owner of the Yankees.

The colonel listened to Barrow denounce the move. Then he listened to the other three beg for the purchase of DiMadge.

"Okay," said the colonel. Thus was the future Yankee Clipper bought from the Seals for $25,000 and four ballplayers. The only concession demanded by Graham was that Joe remain another season in San Francisco.

By then all major league scouts—except Essick and Devine—were moaning. DiMadge batted .398 and cracked out thirty-four homers. He was ready for stardom.

It was delayed slightly in arriving, though. At the spring training camp in St. Pete the future Yankee Clipper was left too long under a diathermy machine and his foot was burned. So he missed the first three weeks of the season. But in his long-awaited debut he hammered out three hits, one a triple. A week later he had his first major league home run and he was just as sensational as advertised. His freshman average was .323 and he had twenty-nine homers.

In his sophomore year of 1937 Jolting Joe achieved his highest homer output, a handsome forty-six, plus a .346 batting average. Two years later his homer total dropped to thirty but his average rocketed up to .381, his all-time high.

It was in 1941, however, that the Yankee Clipper achieved a record that may endure as long as baseball is played. That was the year when he hit safely in fifty-six successive games, a feat so monumental that it earned him the

Most Valuable Player trophy in spite of the fact that Ted
Williams had batted a stupendous .406 that season.

Perhaps the most remarkable part about it was that Joe
had at least one solid, unquestionable hit in each game.
There were freak hits in there, of course. Such was the
grounder he slapped directly at Luke Appling, the White
Sox shortstop, for what should have been an easy out.
Appling swooped in and reached down for the ball. Suddenly it struck a pebble and caromed off his forehead.

Dan Daniel, the official scorer, hesitated. Under ordinary
circumstances he would have instantly raised a finger on
high to signal a hit. But history was being made and Dan
debated momentarily with himself. Slowly and reluctantly
he raised his finger.

"Doggone you, DiMadge," growled Dan. "Hit 'em clean."

But in his next at bat the Jolter removed all doubts. He
slammed a homer.

"The funny thing about that streak," said Joe musingly
many years later, "was that I always got a genuine hit in
every game where I also had a cheap one. And it ended in
spite of the fact that I never hit the ball better than I did
that night against Cleveland."

The Clipper ripped two "doubles" down the third base
line. Each time Ken Keltner, the Indian third baseman,
made acrobatic, impossible stops to rob DiMadge of hits.
And in his last at bat Joe lashed one over second base. The
ball took a queer hop and Lou Boudreau's fast hands turned
it into a double play.

Three times during that streak, particularly grave danger
of interruption arose. Once was against Eldon Auker, the
tricky submarine-baller of the St. Louis Browns. DiMadge
went hitless into the ninth and he was ready to kiss the
streak goodbye. He was the fourth batter of the inning and

someone would have to get on base for him to get as much as a swing. Someone got on base.

Auker set his jaw, determined to halt the rampaging Di-Madge. But the Jolter also set his jaw. He was so over-anxious that he even was willing to violate the rules of all great hitters. He wouldn't wait for a pitch that was a strike. He'd swing at any ball even reasonably near the plate.

He swung at the first pitch. The ball went crackling over the head of the third baseman for a double.

The next close call made the Clipper mad. Johnny Babich was pitching for the Athletics and he refused to meet the challenge head on. He decided he wouldn't throw strikes and would even walk Joe rather than give him a chance to hit. In the first at bat Babich fired in four wide ones. Di-Madge walked.

In the next at bat he served up three balls. It was to be the same thing over again and the Jolter seethed in anger. He looked over for the sign from the bench. Usually, in a three-and-nothing situation the sign is "take," meaning that the batter is not to swing. But DiMadge's heart leaped.

"Good old Joe," he said gratefully to himself. Marse Joe McCarthy, the Yankee manager, had flashed the "hit" sign.

Babich threw. It was a bad pitch, high and outside. But the angry Clipper swung the fat part of his bat around and the ball exploded as it took off. Babich's throwing arm had not even finished its downward descent when a line drive whistled between his legs and into the outfield for a clean hit. As Joe jogged to first he glanced at Babich and laughed. All the color had drained from the pitcher's face, leaving it a sickly green.

Upward the streak mounted until it was one short of the all-time record of forty-four, which had been set almost a half century earlier by Wee Willie Keeler of the old Orioles.

If it was to be tied, it would have to be tied against Heber
Newsome of the Boston Red Sox, and Joe was uneasy. He
never had hit well against Newsome.

But in his first at bat Joe belted a tremendous drive to
the outfield, only to have Stan Spence haul it down. In his
second at bat he hammered one even farther, out near the
monument near the center-field flagpole. And the Red Sox
center fielder happened to be Dominic DiMaggio, Joe's
little brother. What's more, Dom was in Joe's class as an
outfielder. He sprinted furiously and made a supersensa-
tional catch.

When Joe returned to the dugout a sudden flash of humor
overcame him.

"That catch speaks well for the integrity of the game,"
he said wryly. "But Dom didn't have to rub it in that way—
especially when he's coming to my house for dinner tonight."

The Clipper was beginning to despair. Two hard smashes
off Newsome were par for the course as far as he was concerned. With sinking heart he approached the plate again—
and hit a home run.

Not long after the streak had ended, DiMaggio was in
the clubhouse in Washington when his roommate, Lefty
Gomez, called out to him. But suppose we let Joe tell the
story in his own words:

"Lefty says, 'Don't leave without me.' I don't know why
I should wait for him but I say, 'Hurry up, then.' But he
doesn't hurry a bit. I'm ready to leave and he doesn't even
have his shirt buttoned. Everyone else has left the clubhouse. 'Hurry up, you clown,' I say to him. 'You got the
itch or something?' he says to me.

" 'Nuts to you, Gomez,' I tell him. 'I'm going without
you.' I start for the door but he comes running after me,
dressing as he runs. At last we get back to the hotel. I

don't see any of the gang in the lobby, not that it registered on me at the time.

"The next thing I know, Gomez is talking to the desk clerk. 'What now?' I say. 'I want to see Johnny Murphy,' he says. 'Come up to his room with me for just a minute. Honest. Just one minute.' I'm burned up but we've wasted so much time I figure another minute won't hurt. So we go to Murphy's room.

"Gosh, if I live to be a million, I'd never get the kick I got then. The entire Yankee ball club, along with Joe McCarthy, the coaches and the baseball writers were gathered there in a surprise party for me.

"They gave me a sterling silver humidor with '56' lettered on it for the fifty-six-game hitting streak and '91' for the number of hits I'd made during the streak. The signatures of the entire squad were on it, along with a line drawing of me swinging a bat. It was the most beautiful thing I ever saw and the thrill I got from that was the biggest thrill I'll ever get out of baseball."

That incident demonstrates the esteem that DiMadge generated among the Yankees. He never was a holler guy, a speechmaker or a cheerleader. But he was their leader. He did it more by the force of example than anything else—and their respect for him was enormous.

Many years later Joe Page, the left-handed relief pitcher, had turned in one of his extraordinary jobs, striking out slugger after slugger with the bases full. Manager Bucky Harris shook his hand and told him how great he was. The other players crowded around and did the same. So did the writers as they swarmed in for interviews. The praise was unanimous. For Page, however, it was not enough. He drew one writer aside.

"But what did the Big Guy say?" he asked.

The Big Guy, of course, was Jolting Joe. His opinion was the only one that Page valued.

The leadership qualities of the Big Guy were probably never better demonstrated than during the bristling 1949 pennant fight between the Yankees and Red Sox. The previous November a bone spur had been removed from Joe's heel. It was the middle of May before he was able to work out at all and late June before he made his seasonal debut. It was, oddly enough, in a charity game against the Giants, a good spot for experimentation.

The next day the Yankees were to play the red-hot Red Sox in Boston. They went by train. Joe flew up, arriving at game time. In his first at bat he singled, Johnny Lindell walked and Hank Bauer hit a home run. The score was 3 to 0. In his next at bat the Clipper slammed a homer with Phil Rizzuto on base. The Bosox rallied and scored four runs.

With two out and the tying run on base in the ninth, Ted Williams belted a screamer. DiMadge plucked the ball off the center-field fence. The Yanks won, 5 to 4.

A day later the Fenway Millionaires roared off to a 7–1 lead. In the fifth DiMadge clouted a three-run homer. Eventually the Bombers tied the score. DiMadge untied it with a blast out of sight. The Yanks won, 8 to 7.

Vic Raschi was in a squeaker the third day but the pressure was instantly released when DiMadge faced the artful Mel Parnell with two men on in the eighth. His three-run homer caromed off the light tower in left. The Yanks won, 6 to 3.

That's the kind of leadership he always gave the Yankees. Great as Bobby Feller was in his prime, he always had trouble with the Bombers. The reason for it was no mystery. The reason was Jolting Joe.

"I just can't understand it," said Joe one time, shaking

his head in wonderment. "It makes no sense that I should hit a great pitcher like Feller as if I owned him."

Own him DiMaggio did. In one classic prewar game the Yanks went into a ninth inning tie against Feller, 1 to 1. The lone Yankee run was due to a triple by the Clipper. The Bombers filled the bases in the ninth. DiMadge emptied them with a monstrous clout deep into the upper left-field stands.

Baseball has had few clutch performers to match him. He played despite a constant plague of injuries. But he gave his best every moment of every game. Even when he was hobbling in pain during 1947 and insisted on playing anyway, Manager Bucky Harris eagerly consented.

"DiMaggio on one leg is better than most ballplayers on two," he said.

It was true, of course. Yet by the 1951 season retirement had been on his mind with a nagging constancy.

"Baseball isn't fun anymore," he kept saying, a strong hint that he was near the end in spite of a $100,000 salary and constant offers to renew at the same fancy figures. If there had been any doubt about quitting, such doubt was erased when the World Series scouting report that Andy High made for the Dodgers was published. Such reports are hard-boiled and unsentimental to the point of cruelty. A kindly man is High, but his printed report on DiMadge cut him to the core. It read:

> He can't stop quickly and throw hard any more. . . . You can take the extra base on him. . . . He can't run and won't bunt. . . . His reflexes are very slow and he can't pull a good fast ball at all.

Quiet though he was, there was a fierce pride in Di-Maggio. He had been hailed as the epitome of grace, the perfect ballplayer. And then the report exposed him as a hollow shell.

So he turned his back on the $100,000 and quit, a display of his class and character. He was elected to the Hall of Fame, of course. Without him it would have been an empty mockery.

DiMadge was the fellow who carried the baton for the Yankees in their relay race to continued dominance of the sport. Babe Ruth handed it to him, and Jolting Joe, in turn, passed it along to Mickey Mantle. Some relay team!

13

KING GILBERT

Gil Hodges

THE 1952 World Series had been a nightmare for Gil Hodges. The strong man of the Brooklyn Dodgers had been expected to be one of the big boomers against the Yankees. He failed to hit even one home run. But that was the least of it. He also failed to hit even one li'l ol' single. In an epic of futility the muscular first baseman went hitless through the post-season carnival to set a depressing record with a batting average of .000.

It shook him to the core and preyed on his mind all during the winter months. Ordinarily Hodges is a mountain of good nature, mild-mannered and quiet-spoken with a dry wit. His popularity with the other ballplayers has been immense, and the unpredictable Flatbush Faithful treated him with a tender consideration that was unusual in itself.

Big Gil joked about his disastrous World Series all during spring training. However, the harder he tried the worse he got in his batting endeavors during the exhibition schedule. The slump was beginning to become alarming. The season began. In the first month Hodges had only one home run and few other hits. He was benched.

One Sunday in May a heat wave descended on Brooklyn. It was a scorcher, so unseasonably hot that churchgoers wilted. In one Catholic church the Rev. Herbert Redmond was celebrating Mass. He read the announcements and the gospel. The congregation, stirring the sultry air with fans, awaited the sermon. The one that Father Redmond delivered was quite remarkable. Said he from the pulpit:

"It's far too hot for a sermon. Keep the Commandments —and say a prayer for Gil Hodges." He wheeled and returned to the altar.

This was not meant to be a tribute but it was. It had to be. The priest had never met the ballplayer. Like all Brooklynites, however, he was carried away by the wave of sympathy that the plight of Hodges had created. It takes a man of exceptional class and character to inspire such feelings. Yet Gil qualified on every count.

Maybe the prayers helped. Maybe he was aided by the thousands of letters of encouragement that he received. Maybe he was buoyed up by the roars of friendly approval from the crowds. Or maybe he was due to break out of the slump anyway. Whatever it was, Gil returned to the lineup as a full-fledged blaster again. He finished with a .302 average and thirty-one homers.

How good a ballplayer was Hodges in his prime? When Gussie Busch, the millionaire beer baron, bought the St. Louis Cardinals in 1952, he held an organization meeting with his top aides, most of them ranking executives in the Anheuser-Busch empire. Also present was his manager, Eddie Stanky.

"What do we need, Eddie, to win a pennant?" asked Gussie.

"Most of all, Mr. Busch," said the Brat, "we need a first baseman, a slick-fielding power hitter like Gil Hodges of Brooklyn. He had a bad World Series. But if the Dodgers would sell him, he'd come high, maybe as much as $175,000."

"How much?" shrieked the beer moguls. They were horrified. In their business this was a fantastic expenditure and none knew anything about baseball. "What else does Hodges do besides play first base and hit home runs?" said one of them. "At that price he must do other things."

Busch never blinked an eye.

"Let's get him," he said. "In fact, I'll get hold of Walter O'Malley and make the deal myself."

The novice club owner got hold of O'Malley, the most Artful Dodger of all.

"How much do you want for Hodges?" asked Gussie, brisk and businesslike.

"At least $600,000," said O'Malley blandly. Busch almost fell off his chair.

"But don't tempt me," continued O'Malley. "If I ever got rid of Hodges, the Brooklyn fans would hang me, burn me and tear me to pieces. I guess I wouldn't dare let him go at any price."

Many a baseball expert has said that big Gil would have been the greatest first baseman who ever lived if he had had any of the fire and combative urge of a Ty Cobb. But Gil is as amiable as he is large. He gets mad at no one, including himself.

A boxing man once looked him over carefully and got an idea. Gil stands six feet two and weighs a solid 200 pounds. His strength is enormous and he has the reflexes of a jungle cat. He also has the biggest hands ever in baseball, spanning more than eleven inches from thumb tip to the tip of his pinky.

"I could make you the heavyweight champion of the world," said the boxing man.

"Know what?" said Gil, grinning broadly. "I wouldn't even know how to throw a punch. I never hit anyone in my life."

That doesn't mean that timidity overcomes him. Gil is totally unafraid.

When Hodges was first breaking in with the Brooks, an

oversize rookie got into a mix-up with Pee Wee Reese. He went after the Little Colonel with fire in his eyes and mayhem in his heart. Hodges reached out one brawny hand, clutched a fistful of shirt and lifted the 200-pounder off the ground.

"Naughty, naughty," said Gil reprovingly. Then he flung the big fellow gently to the side. Snorting defiance, the huge kid started toward Hodges and suddenly thought better of it. It was just as well. If forced to fight, Gil would have torn him limb from limb.

"He has the fastest hands I ever saw on a ballplayer," was Branch Rickey's estimate and few men have ever seen as many ballplayers as has the Mahatma.

"His hands are so big," said the admiring Pee Wee Reese, "that Gil doesn't even have to wear a glove. He wears one merely because it's the fashionable thing to do."

The willing Gil was always a manager's delight. Whatever position he played, he played well. Furthermore, he was so scrupulous in observing training rules that he never was a worry on that count. He was the ideal.

It was as a nineteen-year-old catcher that Hodges came to the Brooks in 1943 and he got into exactly one game. As a catcher? Don't be silly. They never did do things in so sane and simple a fashion in Ebbets Field. Gil's debut was as a third baseman and hardly was a success. He made no hits but did make two errors. Then he went off to the Marines for three years, spent a season of apprenticeship at Newport News, and returned to the Dodgers as a catcher. He even caught twenty-eight games in 1947, the year that Jackie Robinson broke in as Brooklyn first baseman.

The big juggle came the next season.

"Load the lineup with catchers," sang out Leo Durocher, the Dandy Little Manager, "and win a pennant."

He brought in Roy Campanella from St. Paul to catch.

He stationed Bruce Edwards, a catcher, on third and Gil Hodges, a catcher, on first. Earlier, of course, Robinson had been moved over to second. No pennant was won but the groundwork for many future championships was firmly laid. The cornerstone was Hodges, soon to be recognized as the best first baseman in the business.

First basemen, particularly the great ones, usually stay there for the rest of their careers. But Hodges is so clever, so versatile and so willing that he submitted to a Charlie Dressen brainstorm in 1953. The Brooks had a big, strong kid named Wayne Belardi who could hit right-handed pitchers. So Dressen, anxious to cram more power into his batting order, occasionally stuck Belardi in as a first baseman, shifting Gil to left field.

"Don't you worry a bit with Gil out there?" someone asked.

"I never worry about Gil," snapped the dauntless Dressen. "He's so good he can handle himself anywhere. I just worry about the fences. If one gets in his way, he'll knock it apart."

In 1955 this remarkable handyman also helped out in emergencies as a catcher as well. Two years later he filled in at second. He's played everywhere except as pitcher and shortstop. Oddly enough, he was a shortstop in high school.

One day Reese, a master of the shortstopping position, had been spiked in a play at second. He was stretched out on the trainer's table when Hodges, a dead-pan comic, came over for an inspection. There was no expression on his face as he gave Pee Wee a gentle ribbing. This was the Hodges humor in its most subtle form.

"Dear me," said Gil, clucking in reproval. "Haven't you yet learned how to make that play without being spiked? That's an interesting weakness. What do you say accounts for it—poor reflexes or lack of intelligence?"

Gil Hodges sends one into the stands. One of the most powerful men in the major leagues, Hodges also is a slick-fielding first baseman.

Pee Wee fell for the gag. He flared up.

"If you're so clever," he said, "why didn't you tell me how to make it? You once were a shortstop."

Gil gave him a look of hurt innocence.

"Gee," he said, "I wish I could help you because you honestly need help. It must have been pure instinct with me. It came so naturally to me that I never thought of the mechanics of the play. Even as a kid I could do it perfectly. And you still have trouble with it, you say?"

"Go soak your head, you big lug," said Pee Wee, suddenly realizing that he was being taken.

Gil's drollness was manifested on another occasion. The Dodger plane was whisking the team west when dinner was served, a handsome steak dinner, no less. Harold Parrott, then the traveling secretary, came down the aisle and noticed that big Hodges had pushed his steak aside and was only eating the salad.

"Aren't you hungry?" said Parrott.

"I'm starved," said the very religious Gil. "But today is a day of fast and abstinence. I can't eat meat."

"I've gotten clearance from the bishop," said Parrott. "He told me that Catholics don't have to abstain from meat when they are traveling and nothing else is available."

"How high up is this plane?" asked Hodges, peering up toward the heavens.

"At least 25,000 feet," said Parrott.

"Too close to Headquarters," said Gil, finishing the salad and leaving the steak untouched.

When Hodges was having one of his better seasons in 1951, he had thirty-six homers through August and was already being heralded as the guy who might break Babe Ruth's home run record. But Gil invariably slumps in September and this was no exception. He hit only four in that month (the Babe hammered out seventeen) and finished with forty. Three years later he had forty-two, his all-time high.

By then the experts were beginning to compare the Brooklyn Strong Boy with another durable wonder, Lou Gehrig, the Iron Horse.

"I appreciate the compliment," said Gil in his sly little way. "But Gehrig had one advantage over me."

"What was that?" said the Hodges booster.

"He was a better ballplayer," said Gil.

However, this modest man did achieve one of the great

Gehrig feats, one that even eluded the mighty Babe. He hit four home runs in one game. It happened at Ebbets Field in 1950. As usually is the case, he merely was swinging hard where the ball happened to be and the first three were strictly accidental.

Then Gil went after the fourth with due deliberation and intent. In the seventh inning he faced Bob Hall of the Braves and aimed for the fences. He hit a dribbler on the ground for a scratch single.

"I gave up then," he said afterward. "I was sure I wouldn't get another chance for that fourth homer. But then, I didn't think I could hit three, either."

Luckily for him, the Dodgers batted around in that frame. So he came to bat again, this time against Johnny Antonelli. Hodges put everything into his swing. The ball soared far into the upper left-field stands and the thoughtful fan who caught it returned it to Gil in the clubhouse for a souvenir. He still treasures the ball at his home in Brooklyn.

"Huh," said Reese afterward, giving Gil the needle, "as near as I can see, all you did was prolong the game."

"That I did," said Gil blissfully.

But he's prolonged a lot of games with his homers. So many of them were clutch jobs, too. In fact, Gil holds the National League record for the most grand-slam homers, a gaudy fourteen.

When the Dodgers shifted to Los Angeles, everyone thought that the short left-field fence in O'Malley's Alley would send the Hodges homer total skyrocketing. It didn't, though. He sloughed off to fifteen. There were two main reasons for this.

One was the fence itself. It looked so easy that Gil succumbed to the one temptation he should have resisted. He went shooting for the moon each time and soon had trouble even hitting singles. The second reason was that the shift from his Brooklyn home disrupted his family and Gil has always been the most devoted of family men. He worried and that contributed even more to his ineffectiveness. Lee Walls of the Cubs hit more homers in Los Angeles in eleven games than Hodges did in seventy-seven. That's how bad he was.

The Hodges career is heading toward a close but every homer moves him ever upward with the all-time leaders. If the Dodgers deserted Brooklyn, Hodges did not. He still lives there and his loyal army of supporters in Flatbush still root fervently for him. He has become as enduring an idol in Brooklyn as Zack Wheat and Dixie Walker, two of the few men in Dodger history who never drew as much as one boo from those formidable Brooklyn fans. They even pray for Hodges. No one can ask for more.

14

KING JOHN

Johnny Mize

JOHNNY MIZE was a sailor in the Pacific during World War II, and no gob in the Navy filled out a uniform in more bulging fashion. By 1945 he was stationed on an island with nothing much to do but eat. The war was virtually over, the pressures were off and a fellow was able to start thinking about his future. Since Big Jawn not only was one of baseball's better hitters but one of its deeper thinkers, he pondered long on what destiny might have in store for him.

Two statistical items disturbed him. Presuming he'd be back in the big leagues for the 1946 season, he then would be thirty-three years of age. There was nothing he could do about that. But there was plenty he could do about the other set of figures, his ballooning weight of 250 pounds.

In typical Mize fashion he went to work. A fierce tropical sun beat down with pitiless intensity on that island: it was hot enough to make a stone sweat. The determined Big Jawn wanted far more than that, however. He found a tent. With the flaps down it was an inferno.

Into this torture chamber the large Mr. Mize advanced with grim fixity of purpose. He wore the heaviest clothes he could find. He stretched out on a borrowed wrestling mat and did push-ups, knee bends and every other calisthenic he could remember. It was sheer punishment, a punishment he forced on himself day after day.

By the time the war had ended and Mize was ready for his discharge he had melted away almost forty pounds in his private Turkish bath. He was as trim and frisky when he reported to the New York Giants for the start of the 1946 season as he had been ten years earlier when he was the rookie first baseman of the St. Louis Cardinals. Then he went on to prove that Branch Rickey had made one of the rare miscalculations of the Mahatma's brilliant career as baseball's No. 1 executive.

Rickey theorized that it always was smarter to trade away a ballplayer a year too early than a year too late. The returns were greater that way. Convinced that the usefulness of the Big Cat was on the wane before the start of the 1942 season, the Mahatma traded him to the Giants. But it wasn't until after the 1953 campaign that Johnny, a forty-year-old, hung up his spikes after more than four years of tremendous service with the Yankees. The Giants also had guessed wrong on him and disposed of him too early.

The Big Cat, it would seem, had nine lives. When he was a boy in Demorest, Georgia, he had little interest in baseball. He wanted to become a tennis star, and even won the county singles championship. He also played some baseball but he liked basketball better than baseball and tennis better than both.

When he was in Piedmont High School in 1929, the Piedmont College team was climbing into a bus for an out-of-town game. Last aboard was the coach, who had seen the burly, moonfaced Mize belt for distance in some pickup games. The coach spotted the high school sophomore.

"Why don't you come with us?" he invited. "I have a uniform that will fit and we may need help."

Johnny hit a home run and became a permanent member of the college team. In his droll, dry fashion he commented late in his big league career on that phase of his life.

"That's how I happened to use up my college eligibility," he said, "before I even had graduated from high school."

He could not help attract the attention of the scouts, the most persistent being Frank Rickey, brother of Branch and chief talent appraiser for the Cardinals. Johnny signed and off he went on a tour of the farm clubs to learn his trade. But when he pulled a muscle while performing for Rochester in 1934, he created a suspicion in the mind of the Top Branch. Was Mize injury-prone?

While the Mahatma hesitated, Larry MacPhail made up his mind for him. Laughing Larry was then the boss of the Cincinnati Reds and he offered Rickey $55,000 for the untried and unproven Johnny. The Mahatma couldn't resist that kind of dough. He sold Mize to the Reds.

This phase of the Big Cat's career doesn't even show up in the record books. It was another of his extra lives. At the Cincinnati training camp in Florida the sensation was John Robert Mize.

"The greatest rookie I've ever seen," babbled the Reds' manager, the ever-enthusiastic Charlie Dressen.

But Mize pulled up lame again. Reluctantly MacPhail canceled the transaction and returned him to the Cardinals.

"I wanted to gamble on him," said MacPhail, "but my board of directors overruled me."

The Cards shipped him off to Rochester and Mize proceeded to pull more leg muscles than a spavined horse. Back he came to St. Louis. This was serious and expert medical attention was needed immediately. What was the matter? Dr. Robert Hyland, a master at assaying the ills and ailments of baseball players, made the diagnosis. He gave it to Mize straight, not attempting to soften the blow.

"John," said the doctor, "you have a growth on your pelvic bone and it's giving you all that muscular distress. If you are willing, I can operate. But it's a delicate operation and I can give no guarantees. There even is an outside chance that you will be lame for the rest of your life."

Big Jawn didn't even bat an eye.

"Get the knives ready, doc," he said.

Mize reported at training camp the next spring without a ghost of a chance of making the ball club. Athletes don't recover that fast from serious operations a few months earlier. Besides, the Cardinals still had a holdover first baseman in Rip Collins, one of the charter members of the famed Gas House Gang that had won the world championship two years earlier.

But Big Jawn, a beautifully smooth swinger in spite of his size, soon made a distinct impression on Manager Frank Frisch. He moved into the regular lineup and at the season's end was named Rookie of the Year. He had batted .329 and slammed nineteen homers.

The sophomore jinx would get him in 1937, they said. The Big Cat ignored it, coming into the final day with twenty-four homers.

"Whatsa matter with you, Johnny?" yowled the Cardinal shortstop, a noisy rowdy named Leo Durocher. "I bet you'd hit twenty-five homers and you've only got twenty-four."

"Don't reckon I should let a pal down," drawled the amiable Georgian. "I'll hit you one in my next at bat."

He did for his twenty-fifth. What's more, his batting average was an eye-popping .364 which gave him runner-up honors for the National League batting championship. Joe Medwick won with .374. Two years later Mize won that title himself although with a lower average of .349. It was to trigger off some verbal battles with Branch Rickey.

The most violent one came after the following season of 1940, the year the Big Cat slashed out forty-three homers. No left-handed hitter in National League history ever had hit more. At contract time Mize bounced joyously into

Rickey's office in expectation of a handsome raise. The Mahatma was frowning.

"My boy," said the Mahatma sadly. "I'm afraid I'll have to cut your salary. Your batting average has declined grievously, from .349 to .314."

"But Mr. Rickey," said Big Jawn. "I hit forty-three homers and my lower batting average drove in 137 runs, almost thirty more than when I hit the .349."

They battled away in heated argument before agreeing to a two-year contract.

"One thing I want understood, Mr. Rickey," said Mize, "is that the second year doesn't hold if I'm traded. And I want to be traded. I'm not happy here anymore."

In 1942 Mel Ott, the Giant manager, was trying to assemble a team in his own image: he wanted home run hitters. The grapevine told him he might be able to get Mize. He did. And the Big Cat had a good season with the Giants in 1942 with a .305 average, twenty-six homers and 110 runs batted in. But he also made the discovery that the Polo Grounds, supposedly a homer heaven with its short foul lines, was a dreadful place for a long ball hitter who smashed the ball straightaway and whose power alleys were down the middle—right center, center and left center. Mize would have to change his style a bit and become more of a pull hitter. Fortunately he was so keen a student of the batting art that he was able to do just that.

In his first postwar year of 1946 Big Jawn batted .337 and had twenty-two homers. But he missed a third of the season with injuries. He broke a hand early in August and returned to the lineup on the September day which happened to be Friday the 13th. He broke his foot and was out the rest of the season.

The big home run year was coming up, the year when the Giants set the team record of 221. The leader of those crashing musclemen was Mize. He collected the most money from Hank Gowdy, the paymaster for Ottie, the manager. In spring training that season Ott hit on a novel idea. "Listen, fellows," he said. "I'll pay two dollars for every homer, one dollar for every triple and one dollar for each run batted in. But you'll pay me a deuce whenever you fail to sacrifice a man to second, leave a runner on third or miss a sign."

On the first day Mize walloped a grand-slam homer. Gowdy handed him a $5 bill.

"Don't shortchange me, Hank," said the grinning Big Cat. "Two bucks for the homer and a dollar each for four runs batted in."

"Nope," said Hank. "Five bucks is the most you can get at one time. Ask Ottie. He made the rules."

The competition for stray change added spice to the season and Mize collected $102 on homers alone. He had hit fifty-one and moved into select company. At that time the magic fifty mark had been passed only by Babe Ruth, Jimmy Foxx, Hank Greenberg and Hack Wilson.

The big Giant shakeup came in 1948. At mid-season Horace Stoneham, the owner of the ball club, rocked the baseball world by firing his pet, Ott, and replacing him with the hated refugee from Brooklyn, Leo Durocher. It was then that Mize's days were numbered.

Leo kept nagging Stoneham. "I want my kind of team," he kept insisting. He didn't want the slow homer hitters; he wanted swifties and began plotting in that direction. He looked at Mize with cold appraisal. Not only was the Big Cat heavy-footed afield but had ceased to be a .300 hitter for the first time. He sloughed off to .289 at the season's end.

On the final day that year Mize reported at the Polo Grounds, his huge body racked by a high fever.

"I can't let you play," said the team doctor.

"You can't stop me," said Big Jawn grimly. "I don't want to finish with thirty-nine homers. I want to get forty and I'll quit as soon as I get it."

Mize got his fortieth, thereby tying Ralph Kiner for the home run championship. Then he quit.

Late in August of 1949 the new manager of the Yankees, a certain Casey Stengel, phoned an old buddy, Frank Frisch, and asked for advice. The onetime Fordham Flash was managing the Chicago Cubs and Stengel had been away from the big leagues for so long that he wasn't too sure of himself. He wanted an evaluation from someone he could trust.

"I kin get Mize on waivers, Frank," crackled the Ol' Perfessor. "Do you think he can help me?"

"Yes," said Frisch. "Grab him. Pay whatever you have to pay above the waiver price. But grab him."

Thus did the Big Cat get another life. He was thirty-six years old and near the end. Ironically he wrenched a shoulder and played little for the Yankees in what was left of the regular season. But when the Bombers filled the bases against Ralph Branca in the third game of the World Series, Mize broke a 1–1 tie by lining a screamer off the screen to break the Series wide open.

He hit twenty-five homers for the Yanks in 1950 and was their most valuable part-time operative. In the 1952 World Series he entered the third game as a pinch hitter and slammed a homer.

"That gives me an idea," said Stengel. "You start the next game."

So Joe Collins, who wasn't hitting, was replaced by Mize, who is such an artist that he could hit in his sleep. This was the strategic move that won the World Series for the Yankees. The Big Cat slammed three homers in all—one won a 1–0 game—and batted .400.

A year later Johnny's role was minor. He was forty years of age. At the Yankee victory party the Big Cat introduced his mother to Dan Topping, co-owner of the Yankees.

"Why, you look younger than John," said Topping, too effusively.

Mize looked queerly at his boss, his mind suddenly made up.

"This is the end of the trail for me, Dan," said the Big Cat. "I'm quitting, stepping aside to make room for some young fellow. The Yankees have treated me wonderfully and I have no complaints, just gratitude. Thanks for everything."

It was a graceful exit.

15

KING LAWRENCE

Larry (Yogi) Berra

No sooner had the ink dried on the papers discharging him from the Navy than Lawrence Peter Berra reported to the Yankee Stadium for the first time in his life, still in his sailor suit. Many years later he was describing the incident to a group of wide-eyed rookies as Pete Sheehy, the clubhouse custodian, listened in amusement.

"The first time you saw me, Pete," said Yogi, "I'll betcha never thought I looked like a ballplayer."

"Yogi," said Pete, "you didn't even look like a sailor."

Appearances always have been deceiving as far as Yogi is concerned. The first member of the Yankee organization to make that discovery was Larry MacPhail, then the general manager. Just before the war ended, Mel Ott of the Giants dropped in on the Roaring Redhead.

"I need some catching help, Larry," said Master Melvin. "I've been studying your minor league rosters and you seem to be loaded with good young catchers. The Giants will give you $50,000 for a kid you have in Norfolk. His name is . . ."

Ottie went through the motions of looking up the name.

"His name is Berra," he said innocently.

"Berra?" exclaimed MacPhail. "I never even heard of him. I'll let you know."

But the nimble mind of Laughing Larry worked fast. If this kid is worth $50,000 to the Giants, he reasoned, he must be worth that to us. I'll keep him. That decision was to have considerable effect on the course of baseball history. If the Giants had ever snared Yogi, they would have won a lot more pennants. Without him the Yanks would have won fewer.

Yet even MacPhail was assailed by doubt the first time he set eyes on him. At the war's end many ballplayers checked in at the Yankee front office, some still in their service uniforms. One day MacPhail's secretary notified him that a Mr. Berra was waiting to see him. Here's the way the Redhead described that meeting:

"I was curious about Berra and all I could think of was the fifty grand that Ottie offered for him. In walked Yogi and my heart sank. Here was a funny-looking little guy in a sailor suit. He had a homely face, no neck and the build of a sawed-off weight lifter. My first thought was: Did I turn down $50,000 for this? Never have I seen anyone who looked less like a ballplayer."

But in Yogi's first game as a Yankee in September of 1946, he hit a home run. More than fifteen years later he still is at it, one of baseball's most beloved characters, three times the Most Valuable Player in the American League.

It was tough in the beginning, though. If Yogi did not have such monumental good nature, the bench jockeys would have ridden him out of baseball with their cruel jibes.

The favorite gesture of derision was for an enemy player to clutch the top of the dugout with one hand and let his body swing while scratching himself with his free hand.

"Hey, Yog, look," the needler would shout. "Do you still sleep in a tree?" Then would come the eerie cry of Tarzan summoning the apes.

"I don't hafta hit with my face," Yogi would reply.

The ribbing faded away as soon as the other ballplayers got to know him. Behind that craggy exterior they found a

man who was sweet and gentle and kind. He was naïve, blundered into the wrong words and did some of the darndest things. Yet he compensated for his lack of formal education with a shrewd native intelligence.

There was one occasion when a double play was made backwards. It was so unusual that the Yankees remained in the field, the next hitter moved toward the batter's box and the umpire wheeled around to dust off the plate. Only Yogi acted as though the inning was over. He rolled the ball back toward the mound and headed toward the dugout.

Suddenly, he raced back, grabbed the ball and looked around wildly, convinced by the reactions of everyone else that he had made a mistake. Not until then did everyone realize that the inning was truly over. The Yankee players jogged in. The enemy jogged out. Certainly the play had been involved and unusual. But the fact was inescapable: Only Yogi was smart enough to know what it all was about.

In a way the man is a complete paradox. In the second game of the 1956 World Series the Bronx Bombers squared off against big Don Newcombe of the Dodgers. They filled the bases in the second inning and up stepped Yogi. He gracefully hammered a pitch into Bedford Avenue for a grand-slam homer.

The angry giant went to the showers and left the ball park. The parking lot attendant spoke insultingly to Newcombe and, it was alleged, big Don struck him. Not until the seventh and deciding game did Newk return to the firing line, still beset by doubt and self-recrimination.

With a runner on base in the first inning the huge right-hander threw with such blinding speed that he struck out Mickey Mantle. Up to the plate stepped Yogi and clouted another one into Bedford Avenue for a home run.

Newcombe was a shaken man when he finally came to

bat. Was it a fat pitch he'd fed Berra? Here was a tormented man, one who could have been destroyed instantly by one unkind word. No one was in a better spot to utter that unkind word than Yogi as he crouched behind the plate with the giant pitcher at bat.

"That was a real good pitch I hit, Newk," said Yogi, trying to comfort him. "A real good pitch."

"Thanks, Yog," said Newcombe gratefully.

An inning later Yogi stopped being so considerate. Again Newk fanned Mantle with a runner on base. Again the midget muscleman, Berra, powdered one over the fence for a homer and Newcombe didn't linger around to find out if it was "a real good pitch." It didn't matter anymore.

Yogi is easily the most conversational catcher in the business. He talks to the batters, the umpires and anyone else within earshot.

"There's lotsa reasons why I gotta keep usin' Mister Berra as a ketcher," Casey Stengel once explained with a broad wink. "Not only does Mister Berra help me manage but he talks to all the hitters which is how I kin find out what's goin' on inside the other ball clubs. When I use him in the outfield I lose my pipeline and he's very unhappy because he don't have nobody to talk to."

If the ballplayers enjoy Yogi's conversations, the umpires don't. At least they don't when he second-guesses them on balls and strikes.

One day the 280-pound Cal Hubbard was umpiring behind the plate. Yogi kept growling every time a ball was called.

"Come on, Cal," grumbled Yogi for the umpteenth time. "That was a strike." The umpire halted play and whipped off his mask.

"Yogi," he said, "there's no sense in both of us umpiring

this game together. Since I'm getting paid to do it, I have to stay here. But you don't. One more squawk out of you and away you go."

Yogi shut up.

"Yogi is the last of the playing umpires," cracked Joe Garagiola, the radio broadcaster who has been Berra's life-long friend.

They grew up together as next-door neighbors on the Hill, the Italian section of St. Louis, and eventually formed a reversible battery on the Stags. When Joe pitched, Yogi caught. When Yogi pitched, Joe caught. They even went to their first big league tryout camp together, that of the St. Louis Cardinals.

Garagiola was signed as a catcher. Yogi's looks were against him; he was bypassed. That's how it happened that Joe became the rookie star of the Cardinals in 1946 before Yogi even reached the major leagues. But once Berra made it, he was to outlast and outshine his buddy.

While Joe was cracking the big time, Yogi was finishing his apprenticeship with Newark, the top Yankee farm team. There he was assigned to room with the erudite Bobby Brown, who already had begun his postgraduate studies at the Tulane Medical School. They were an odd pair: Brown was tall, handsome, debonair, brilliant, polished and edu-cated; Berra was none of those things.

One night in their hotel room each was busy reading. Yogi was poring over comic books; Bobby was studying a ponderous medical tome. The doctor-to-be closed his book. Yogi looked up.

"Hey, Bobby," he asked, "how did your book come out?"

It was in 1949 that rumors got around that Yogi had fallen in love. The Yankee ballplayers were startled. Berra had never paid attention to girls and seemed to spend most of his spare time on the road going to cowboy movies with

Phil Rizzuto. So the question was put to him point-blank. "Why not?" said Yogi defensively. "I'm human, ain't I?" He married a real beauty, Carmen Short, with Joe Garagiola serving as best man. The newlyweds departed to St. Petersburg, the Yankee spring training base in Florida, for their honeymoon. It was there that a dazed Yogi learned about the depth of true love.

Driving to the ball park one day, he reached into the glove compartment of his car, taking his eyes off the road. He ran into a palm tree. The accident was not serious.

"Gee," said Yogi to his teammates the next day. "Carmen was more upset about what happened to me than what happened to the car. Gee."

That also was the year when Stengel took over as manager of the Yankees. Berra had served two seasons under Bucky Harris and had made little progress as a fielder, although his hitting was impressive. What disturbed the experts most was that Yogi rarely waited for a pitch to come whistling through the strike zone. He would swing at anything, including pitches off his ear or his shoetops. What's more, he could hit them, becoming the most proficient badball hitter since Joe Medwick.

"If I had to give back all my bad-ball hits," Yogi was to say in later years, "I'd really be in trouble."

But in his freshman year of 1947 Harris was trying to correct Berra of this flaw.

"Think when you go to bat, Yogi," he exhorted. "Think, think, think."

With that advice ringing in his ears, Yogi went to bat and struck out. He returned to the bench grumbling.

"How can a guy think and hit at the same time?" he asked.

But Yogi did so much thoughtless hitting that Bucky couldn't keep him out of the lineup. The trouble was he didn't know where to play him. He tried him as a catcher and he tried him as an outfielder. In neither post was Yogi a rousing success. He opened as a catcher in the 1947 World Series and the Dodgers did everything but steal his chest protector. Reluctantly Bucky benched his stumpy little hero. Then he put him in as a pinch hitter and Berra slammed a home run. Back into the lineup he came, this time as an outfielder. He was to be in both spots during the 1948 season.

And along came Stengel. The shrewd Casey brought with him as a coach the greatest of all Yankee catchers, Bill Dickey.

"He's yours," said Stengel to Dickey at St. Pete, gesturing in the direction of Berra. "It's up to you to make a catcher out of him."

The sharp eyes of Dickey solved the problem immediately. Yogi's trouble was with his feet. He was crouching wrong and stepping wrong, always off balance. Corrections were made.

"Bill is learnin' me his experience," explained Yogi in a remark which was to become a classic.

He "learned him good," a Berraism which should be translated into "he taught him well." Yogi became a slick and polished catcher. After that all he ever stumbled over were words.

Not long after his marriage, he returned to visit his mother on the Hill. Neighbors gathered around. One began to chide him on marrying a girl of German descent instead of one of the dark-eyed signorine. He asked Yogi if he considered that fair.

"They had their chance," said Yogi thoughtfully.

It was in St. Loo that he uttered a line that will forever remain the gem in the collection. They held a Yogi Berra Night in old Sportsman's Park and thousands of his old neighbors and friends, plus countless new friends, gathered to pay him tribute. Yogi has no gift for words anyway and the sight of the roaring multitude made him freeze. He spoke only one stuttering line—and fluffed it.

"I wanna thank you fans for makin' this night *necessary*," he croaked into the microphone.

It is only under the strongest compulsion that Yogi will ever consent to make a speech. They usually are the shortest speeches on record, and Jackie Farrell of the Yankee front office usually writes them out in advance.

They once were at a dinner when Yogi reached over to study his lines. Then he nudged Farrell.

"Is this the way I start?" he said. "Ain't there some way I begin this?"

"Sure," said Farrell. "You begin with the usual: Mr. Toastmaster, Honored Guests—oh, oh. There's a priest on the dais—Reverend Father, Ladies and Gentlemen."

"Write it out," ordered Yogi. Farrell wrote it out. As dessert was being served, Jackie felt a poke in his ribs.

"Jackie," whispered Yogi, "the priest just left to hear confessions." He pointed to the words of introduction. "We're loused up again," he said.

Yogi's enthusiasms run high. When he bought a house for the first time, he was bubbling over as he arrived at the Yankee Stadium.

"What a house!" he exclaimed. "It's full of rooms."

His latest mansion is even more full of rooms, plus a huge yard that happens to be "full of trees."

Carmen decorated it tastefully, of course, and one of the showpieces of the living room is a handsome piano. Yogi was raving about it to John Drebinger, the baseball expert of *The New York Times*.

"That's wonderful," said Drebbie, a pianist himself. "I hope you and your family get a lot of pleasure out of it."

"The trouble is," said Yogi sadly, "that no one knows how to play it."

"Too bad," said Drebbie.

"I'd like to ask a favor of you, Dreb," said Yogi. "How about comin' out to the house some night and showin' me how it works?"

One of the major disappointments for the vast army of Berra fans was the way the 1960 World Series ended. Yogi had apparently won the championship for the Bombers late in the game, hooking a three-run homer just inside the foul pole.

The little man completed his swing, took a few fearful steps and just stood, staring openmouthed at the flight of the ball. Then he seemed to leap twelve feet in the air as if just bounced off a trampoline. He came down into a grotesque dance of unrestrained joy and danced all the way around the bases. Then the Pirates snatched Yogi's hero role away from him when Bill Mazeroski homered in the ninth to end it all.

A significant statement was made during that Series by Bob Friend, the Pittsburgh pitcher.

"Yogi is the most relaxed hitter I ever saw or faced," he said. "In spite of all the great things he has accomplished over the years he's lost none of his humility and none of his niceness. He's truly one of nature's noblemen."

What makes the pitchers fear Yogi so much as a batter is that he seems to get better and sharper as a game progresses. Perhaps that's why he has made so many hits in the clutch, the late-inning wallops that catch the headlines.

Yogi is quite conscious of his limitations as a subject of interviews. If he knows the interviewer well enough, he sometimes will make a plea.

"Fix it up so that it comes out good," he will ask. "Just don't let me sound like too much of a dope."

Yogi does all right in interviews, his fears to the contrary. Usually it's a spontaneous remark that worms its way into columns and into lasting repetition.

In 1955 the Brooklyn Dodgers defeated the Yankees in the World Series. Here was an earthshaking event, the first championship for the Brooks in all recorded history. Being novices at this sort of thing, the deliriously happy Dodgers did an unprecedented thing. They swarmed into the Yankee dressing room to seek congratulations. None was more ecstatic than Jackie Robinson.

Yogi was sitting glumly in front of his locker when Robbie rushed over to shake his hand. Yogi looked up.

"Hello, Jackie," he said. "What's new?"

There always seems to be something new with Lawrence Peter Berra. The inherent class of this lovable little guy shines through constantly, even when he trips over his own tongue.

16

KING HENRY

Hank Greenberg

DURING the 1945 World Series a reporter for some high school newspaper did the impossible. In some mysterious fashion that no one ever was able to explain, he contrived to get on the playing field during batting practice. Not only did this brash youth mingle with the genuine, credential-bearing baseball writers, but he didn't hesitate to ask questions of the ballplayers.

He was polite enough, though. He spoke to a few lesser lights and then headed toward the biggest star on the premises, Hank Greenberg. The Detroit slugger had been in the Army for four years, and had been discharged just in time to give the Tigers the lift they needed to win the pennant. But it had been an agonizing experience as Hammerin' Hennery punished muscles that had grown unused to such violent strain. By World Series time, Hank already had started to buckle.

The kid walked over to him, pencil poised over notebook. He asked one question and got the shortest interview on record.

"Tell me, Mr. Greenberg," he said brightly. "When the World Series is over, what do you intend to do?"

"Collapse," said Hank.

The situation wasn't that bad, of course. But it did have overtones that the big slugger, a highly intelligent man, already had recognized. He was edging toward the end of his playing days. Four long years had been peeled off his career and he was almost thirty-five years old. Baseball had not come easily or naturally to him. He was a self-made ballplayer and self-made ballplayers rust away more quickly from disuse than do those with inborn skills.

He played one more season with Detroit and then was unceremoniously sold to the Pittsburgh Pirates in the other league. It was a jolt to his pride. This meant that the rest of the American League had declined to claim him, letting him depart on waivers.

Hank refused to go at first but then reconsidered. The biggest contribution he made to the Buccaneers doesn't even show in the record books. He made a great home run hitter out of his roommate, Ralph Kiner. But he himself had an indifferent season by his own high standards and called it a career, although he was offered an $80,000 salary to continue.

It had been a notable career, though, for the big kid from the sidewalks of New York. He could serve as a model, an example and an object lesson for every boy in America. He started out with virtually no talent, but by dint of hard work and intelligent concentration gained a place among the immortals in the Hall of Fame at Cooperstown.

Hank was cursed with two left feet when he first tried to play baseball. As a fielder he just wouldn't do. Nor could he hit a curve. So lacking was he in natural ability, it seemed impossible that he'd ever make the grade. But this solidly constructed giant (six feet four and 215 pounds) never gave up—and never lost faith in himself. If ever a man lifted himself by his own bootstraps, he was Henry Benjamin Greenberg.

He slaved to perfect himself. Morning after morning he'd get out to the ball park early. Being a quick man with a dollar bill, he would hire any attendants he could corral to

help him learn the finer points of baseball. For endless hours
he practiced fielding, hitting and throwing. And even when
he departed from his original role of a tall, ungainly, crude
workman into a polished star, he still spent hours in either
eliminating weaknesses or in strengthening his strong points.

"When I was a kid I used to play ball eight hours a day
for nothing," he once explained with a smile. "So why
shouldn't I do the same thing when I'm getting paid for it
as a professional?" Why not, indeed?

In the ordinary course of events Greenberg would have
been a Yankee. He was born in New York, lived in the
Bronx and attended James Monroe High School where he
was a star in baseball, basketball and—of all things—soccer.

One of the few scouts who saw any possibilities in this
awkward giant was Paul Krichell, the demon Yankee scout.
He thought he had the inside track because Hank was like
most Bronx kids. He worshiped Babe Ruth and frequently
bought a bleacher seat to watch his idol. But he also studied
Lou Gehrig. That finished any notions he might have had to
enlist under the Yankee banner. The Iron Horse looked
indestructible, as if he could go on forever. There never
would be room on the Bombers for Hank Greenberg, first
baseman.

So he signed with the Tigers for $9,500 and insisted that
he could not be farmed out to any team below Double A
(those teams are now Triple A) classification. He went to
Hartford, one rank lower, at the suggestion of the Tigers.
This also was too fast for him.

"Forget about that clause in the contract," he told his
bosses. "Send me anywhere I can learn to play baseball."

It was an intelligent and realistic appraisal of the situation. Even as a teen-ager Hank was smart enough to know
that he would flunk out by sticking blindly to the terms of
his contract. There were no shortcuts; he would have to

work his way up from the bottom—and hard work never scared Hank Greenberg. In his fourth season as a professional he had made the big leagues. What's more, he batted .301 as a freshman. A year later he was a star with a .339 average and twenty-six homers. The year was concluded with the flourish of the 1934 World Series against the swaggering Gas House Gang of St. Louis.

The statistics might seem to show that Hank had a good Series because his average was .321. But four of those hits came when neither of the Dean brothers was pitching. He fanned nine times, often in the clutch, and Dizzy Dean made life miserable for him.

By the time the Tigers and the Cardinals reached the seventh game, Ol' Diz was having a ball. He had a 11–0 lead when Greenberg came to bat again. The self-confessed Great Man walked off the mound to second base where Frank Frisch, the fiery manager of the Gas Housers, was stationed.

"Hey, Frankie," drawled Diz, jerking a thumb toward Greenberg at the plate. "Kin this guy hit anything at all?"

"He sure can," snarled the grim and serious Flash. "He murders a fast ball on the outside."

So Dean gave Hammerin' Hennery a fast ball on the outside. Greenberg lashed a sizzling single to center.

"You're right," said the imperturbable Diz. "I wuz jes' beginnin' to think he couldn't hit nuthin' at all."

"Stop horsing around," yowled the anguished Flash. "Have you forgotten, you big meathead? We're in the World Series. If you don't stop your clowning, I'll yank you."

"Hmmmm?" hmmmed Diz as he returned to the hill. "They ain't nobody yankin' Ol' Diz when he got hisself an 11–0 lead."

He was eminently correct, of course. Ol' Diz got his 11–0 shutout and the Gas House Gang won the World Series.

The Greenberg homer output mounted to thirty-six in 1935 when he was elected the Most Valuable Player in the American League. But in 1936 he broke his wrist in a collision at first base and was out for most of the season. Back he came a year later with forty homers—and then came the big assault.

For Hank 1938 was a strange season. He started in a slump and stayed there. Although he couldn't hit singles, which provide the solid floor in the construction of any batting average, he still could hit homers. There was one nine-game stretch when he got only five hits. All five were home runs.

But after the All-Star break the Greenberg bat became hot. He ripped off singles and doubles as well as four consecutive homers in a two-game span. Suddenly the fans began to watch with growing intentness. Hammerin' Hennery was running ahead of the Babe record pace until he went into September with forty-six, three more than Ruth had made at a corresponding time.

"I revered the Babe so much and was in so much awe of him," Hank was to say in later years, "that I still didn't think I had a chance of breaking his record until I hit my fifty-seventh and fifty-eighth in the same afternoon. I still had five games to go. For the first time all season the thought flashed through my mind, 'I can do it.' "

He didn't, though. His first foe was Bobo Newsom, wise and efficient. Bobo was shooting for his twentieth victory and took no chances anyway. He gave Hank nothing. Hank hit nothing. A day later a jittery rookie, Howie Mills, was too nervous to get anything over the plate for the big slugger. He walked Hennery three times and accidentally got only one throw within range. Hank crashed it into the stands—foul by inches.

The scene shifted to Cleveland. Another cagey pitcher, Denny Galehouse, also gave Hank nothing. Time was running out. The Saturday game was canceled to provide a closing day doubleheader. That day dawned, dark and threatening. Black clouds scudded across the skies and visibility was bad.

And who should be the Cleveland pitching nominee but Bobby Feller whose fast ball couldn't be seen even in bright sunshine. Hank was not the only Tiger who couldn't see it that day. Rapid Robert set a record of eighteen strikeouts, two by Greenberg.

The second game of the twin bill began late and there were no arc lights to cut into approaching darkness. Johnny Humphries, another fast baller, was the Indian pitcher. The game should have been called before it actually was. But George Moriarty, the umpire in chief, was fond of Greenberg and did not want to foreshorten his opportunities. By the sixth inning, though, he had no choice.

"I'm sorry, Hank," said Moriarty. "I'll have to call the game. This is as far as I can go."

"That's all right, George," said Hank. "This is as far as I can go, too."

Thus did his homer bid end at fifty-eight.

The 1941 season was a short one for Greenberg. It lasted only nineteen games. Then he enlisted in the Army. But his farewell to baseball was a warming one. The Tigers were playing the Yankees and Tiny Bonham was pitching. In his first two at bats Greenberg exploded home runs.

As he took his position in the field, he started to think and calculate. He held the record for two home runs in one

game but he never had hit three. Sudden realization struck
him that he had just clouted the 248th and 249th homers of
his career. What a wonderful exit it would be, he thought, if
he could wind up with three homers for the first time, the
third also being his 250th.

Here's the way he tells the story:

"I immediately became intensely interested in hammering one into the stands. That's a funny thing about baseball.
In my first two trips to the plate I'd never given it a thought,
just taking my cut without consciously trying for the home
run. Yet I'd connected both times.

"As I stepped to bat in the last half of the eighth we had
the game won and everybody in the park was pulling for
me to finish with a homer, myself included. Atley Donald
was pitching for the Yankees and the bases were full. What
a perfect spot that was! Frank Merriwell himself couldn't
have picked a nicer way to leave baseball before going off
to war.

"Donald didn't have a thing. He was wild and he tossed
up three balls. I didn't want a walk and I was both surprised and amused to discover that even Bill Dickey, the
Yankee catcher, was rooting for me. The next pitch came
as large as a balloon. I missed it. I swung again and missed.
Then came the final pitch, the payoff for my home-run
ambitions. I really took a belt at that one. A home run?
No. A triple? No. A double—but why string it out? I fanned
most magnificently."

On July 1, 1945, four years and fifty-five days after he
had made homer No. 249, Capt. Hank Greenberg shed his
Army uniform for a Tiger one. By way of celebrating his
return, he hit a home run. It was a long time in coming but
he finally got No. 250.

More important, perhaps, was No. 262. It came on the

final day of the 1945 season when the Tigers needed just one more victory to clinch the pennant from the Washington Senators. But they were on the road to failure on that dark, misty afternoon. They trailed by a run in the ninth, filled the bases with one out and rested all their hopes on the bat of Hank Greenberg. He hit a grand-slam home run and the Tigers were in the World Series again.

Perhaps no man in baseball ever went farther on less natural ability than did Hank Greenberg, the Hall of Fame immortal. He demonstrated to the youth of America that hard work, determination and perseverance can take a man to the top.

17

KING WILLIE

Willie Howard Mays

THE New York Giants sent Eddie Montague on a scouting expedition to inspect Alonzo Perry, the first baseman on the Birmingham Black Barons. Montague made the trip but let himself become distracted. He just couldn't take his eyes off the nineteen-year-old boy who was patrolling center field. He forgot all about Perry and kept watching the kid outfielder, a certain Willie Mays.

"Once I saw Mays," reported Montague, "it was hard to look at anyone else. He hit line drives with power to all fields. He had the quick hands of Joe Louis in his prime. He had a great arm and was a jackrabbit on the bases. Here was a kid who had everything." So the Giants bought him for $14,000 and sent him to Trenton, the Class B farm club.

The next spring Leo Durocher whisked over to the Sanford minor league base of the Giants for a personal look. Leo the Lip is loud and brassy and emphatic. When his enthusiasms are aroused he can fling superlatives better than a Hollywood press agent. After his first sight of Willie the Wonder, he came back, babbling almost to the point of incoherence.

During the early stages of the season the Giants floundered. The Dandy Little Manager knew he had a far better ball club than it appeared to be and he is far too impatient to let nature take its course. So he reached out

to the Minneapolis farm club where the 'Mazing Mays was rocking the league with a batting average of .477.

A fortnight after his twentieth birthday, Willie was wearing a Giant uniform, bewildered and scared. He laced the ball well and cracked enough line drives to merit a hatful of hits. But his luck was atrocious. All sped straight into the gloves of fielders. This just added to his bewilderment and to his dismay.

He was in tears one afternoon when he walked into the office of Durocher, the little martinet.

"Boss man," sobbed Willie, "I'm hurtin' the team. You better bench me or send me back to the minors."

Leo can be harsh and unfeeling, but this was not one of those times. He draped a fatherly arm around Willie's shoulders.

"Don't you worry, son," he said and there was almost a note of tenderness in his brassy voice. "You're not going anywhere but here. Just keep swinging because you're my center fielder even if you don't get a hit for the rest of the season."

Mays emerged shiny-eyed. The crisis had passed. What's more, his relationship with Durocher took on a new dimension. Leo assumed a father image to the lonely boy, replacing the father he never knew. Leo's word was law and the slightest suggestion became a command. Willie idolized his manager and, for that matter, Leo idolized Willie.

The first hit the Wonder made in the big leagues was characteristic of him. It was made off Warren Spahn, a home run that soared high over the roof of the left-field stands at the Polo Grounds. He was a success from the start, an electrifying ballplayer who teemed with color and class.

He was a mascot of sorts. His teammates were captivated by this laughing, likable kid with the shrill voice and the bubbling humor that left everyone with a warm feeling. He gave life and vibrancy to the entire ball club, merely by being himself. And he lit the spark which led to the Little Miracle of Coogan's Bluff, the unbelievable closing rush which carried the Giants to a pennant after trailing the Dodgers by thirteen and a half games in mid-August.

Although Willie's hitting tailed off near the season's end, he still finished with a respectable .274 and twenty homers. He was a runaway choice as the Rookie of the Year.

Some of the plays he made left spectators gasping. One day he produced a double catch. He came racing in from deep center and made a headlong dive for the ball as his hat flew off. With his glove hand he speared the ball and with his right hand he caught the cap. Reflexes? He had twice the normal allotment.

During that season an endless debate began: Which was Willie's greatest play? One gem that was burned into memory was against the Dodgers. The score was tied in the eighth with runners on first and third, one man out and Carl Furillo at bat.

Furillo rifled a line drive to right center. Perhaps it would go for a double. But Billy Cox, the runner on third, could afford to play it safe. He was certain to score whether or not the ball was caught. So he tagged up on third.

Willie streaked like a gazelle over the Polo Grounds turf. With a last, desperate leap he collared the ball. But he was running away from the play at the plate. He would have to stop, reverse his body and make the throw. Not Willie, however. Baseball instinct permeates every fiber of his being.

He did not stop and make the play in orthodox fashion, which was clockwise. He just spun counterclockwise and let go a throw. The ball came at Wes Westrum, the catcher, as if it had been launched from a cannon. It didn't bounce

in, as outfield throws are supposed to do. It came on the
fly. From deep right center Willie the Wonder had thrown
a strike. The astonished Cox was tagged out.

Willie's own comment was priceless.

"That was the perfectest throw I ever made," he said
simply.

Willie was a happy mixture of boyish naïveté and brash
confidence when he joined the Giants. His bubbling good
nature acted as a shield to protect him from the jokesters
and the needlers on both his own and the other teams. His
quick laughter disarmed them. Furthermore, his performances earned their respect.

The energy of the twenty-year-old was boundless. During batting practice he couldn't just stand around and wait
his turn like a normal ballplayer. He had to be doing something. So he'd field balls for the fungo hitters, demonstrating
reflexes so sharp that he almost was like a magician doing
sleight-of-hand tricks with a baseball.

Once the big league game was over at the Polo Grounds,
he would return to his apartment in Harlem only long
enough to grab a quick meal. Then he'd be out on the
streets, playing stickball with the neighborhood kids.

Measured by baseball statistics, Willie was one of the
lesser heroes in the Little Miracle of Coogan's Bluff and in
the World Series that followed. But he had made his mark
in other ways. Rich was the promise he held out for the
future.

"I wouldn't trade Willie Mays," barked out the enthusi-
astic Durocher, "for any player in baseball—including Ted
Williams and Stan Musial." Leo the Lion meant every word
of it, too.

In May of 1952 the blow fell. Willie the Wonder was
tapped for the Army.

"It's gonna be lonesome around here without Willie," said Leo the Lip mournfully. "He's the heart and soul of the ball club."

The Giant players gave him a portable radio as a going-away present. Willie was so choked up with emotion that tears welled into his eyes. But when he saw those smiling, friendly faces around him, he relaxed. Triumphantly he raised a fist.

"Jes' hold 'em, fellers," he said, "till I get back."

Without the 'Mazing Mays, however, the Giants could hold no one. They challenged the Dodgers for a while but the spark was gone. When the season still had a month to go, Charlie Dressen, manager of the Brooks, issued his classic statement.

"The Giants is dead," he said.

They were. They were even deader in 1953 when they faded to fifth place. Obviously everyone was marking time, waiting for Willie's return. It came in early March of 1954 at the spring training camp in Phoenix, Arizona. He had ridden the plane all night and an intrasquad game was in progress when he arrived. He disrupted it.

Durocher came rushing toward the runway and enveloped his pet in a bear hug. Players, photographers and reporters swarmed around. Eventually the game was resumed.

In the fifth inning Willie went to bat as a pinch hitter. He slammed a three-run homer over the fence. Then he went into the field and saved the victory with two super-sensational catches.

"He means the pennant for us," boasted Leo. "He was just learning when he left us. This year I figure he'll bat about .280 and have twenty-five homers."

The Dandy Little Manager was right about the pennant but he was far short of the mark as far as the Mays personal

statistics were concerned. Willie didn't hit .280. He won
the National League batting championship with .345. He
didn't hit twenty-five homers. He belted forty-one. And he
won the Most Valuable Player trophy in a breeze.

Perhaps that one season best demonstrates the untapped
potential of Willie the Wonder and best illustrates his enormous versatility as a hitter. By the time of the All-Star
interlude Mays had thirty-one homers and by the end of
July he had thirty-six. He was well ahead of that noted
measuring rod, "Babe Ruth's record pace."

But the Giant pitching staff then began to get involved
in squeakers. Frequent singles became more necessary to
victory than infrequent home runs. Willie cut down on his
power and began to spray out the hits. On the last day of
the season he came up with just enough to edge out his
teammate, Don Mueller, for the batting championship.

Then came the World Series against the Cleveland
Indians. In the first game the Wonder made the catch to
end all catches. It was so unbelievable that it almost seemed
to be an optical illusion. With two men on base the muscular
Vic Wertz crashed a tremendous shot to deepest center,
and no field in the majors had a deeper center field than the
Polo Grounds.

Willie wheeled at the crack of the bat and raced toward
the bleacher wall, 460 feet from home plate. He ran and
ran and ran. Presumably he had eyes in the back of his
head. There is no other explanation. Suddenly Willie stuck
out his glove and the ball darted over his left shoulder,
plunking into the pocket of the glove. The 'Mazing Mays
had just made one of the greatest catches in baseball history.

The stunned silence of the crowd was splintered by
shrieks of astonished disbelief. And millions of television
viewers all over the country reacted the same way. Fortu-

nately for posterity this electrifying feat was captured on film and on tape, perpetual proof that the Wonder had achieved the impossible.

But to baseball purists the best part of this play was not even noticed by anyone except a full-fledged expert. It came a split second after that implausible catch and demonstrated how deep-seated is the Mays baseball instinct. In an unbroken flow of motion Willie jammed on the brakes, wheeled and fired a prodigious throw back to the infield in order to keep the base runners from getting any scoring ideas.

Willie was a bewildered young man in 1955. Fame and acclaim confused him, intruding on his simple way of life. Durocher kept spoiling him like an overindulgent father, and Giant teammates were starting to resent the way they were being treated like stepchildren, with Willie the favorite son. A session of winter baseball started him out tired and dulled his skills.

In June he was benched, briefly. In August he missed a shoestring catch and failed to chase the ball. Fans booed him for the first time. But Willie still gathered himself together for a closing rush that lifted his batting average to .319, despite a sudden yen for distance clouting. Reversing his procedure of the previous year he went for homers instead of singles to wind up with his top total, fifty-one.

"Willie had an off year," said Giant fans. But did he? The statistics would seem to prove otherwise.

Then came the blow which rocked the Wonder right out of Wonderland. Horace Stoneham, the owner of the Giants, had taken as much of Durocher as he could stand. He let go of Leo and replaced him as manager with Bill Rigney, who liked Mays but did not regard him with the same rapturous infatuation that the Lip did. His attitude was different.

"Willie is just another ballplayer," said Rig brusquely. "He'll be treated the same as any other member of the squad."

Willie was lost. He had no Durocher to coax and con and cajole him. He had no Durocher to insult him good-naturedly, provoke him to laughter and spur him to heroics. Willie hit .296, although he did have thirty-six homers.

If this treatment did nothing else, however, it forced Mays to grow up. It gave him maturity. By 1957 Willie was again a great and exciting ballplayer, the idol of the Polo Grounds clientele. He hit .333 with thirty-five homers and was headed toward still unexplored peaks.

Then came another shattering blow, although Willie weathered this in style. The Giant franchise was shifted from New York to San Francisco and the Wonder was leaving his friends, the fans and the writers. He had to prove himself all over again, and fate was unkind to him.

The new fans were expecting a superman. By some quirk, however, he made all his sensational plays on the road and nothing but routine plays in San Francisco. So the spectacular rookie, Orlando Cepeda, became the pinup boy of these new Giant fans. Willie's .347 batting average and twenty-nine homers were ignored.

Life which was one sweet dream for a young Willie Mays became harsh reality for an older one. An unhappy marriage added to its complications. He was an $80,000-a-year ballplayer who had a lot more fun when he was working for the $7,500 minimum. That's when he could play stickball with the kids in the streets and shoot pool with cronies in the corner billiard academy.

To San Franciscans he's a legend they've read about but have rarely actually seen with their own eyes. It's uncanny how that plot constantly kept unfolding. A prize example came in a game with the Braves in May of 1961. Naturally enough, it took place in Milwaukee.

In Willie's first at bat he hit a homer. In his second he slammed a liner to deepest center. It was caught. In his next two he crashed out home runs. Once more he stepped to the plate and the thought flickered briefly through his mind that four homers in one game would be a historic achievement. Only eight men had ever done it.

"I can't do it," said Willie to himself as he stepped into the batter's box against Don McMahon.

Willie swung. Thrills tingled up and down his spine. He knew while the ball was still in flight that he had done it.

"Imagine me doin' that!" he shouted in glee as he rounded first. He kept repeating the sentence in a dancing, joyous and laughing trip around the bases, his fourth homer in one game.

Willie Howard Mays, Jr., may be the best ballplayer of his generation. If San Francisco fans are reluctant to believe it, the Polo Grounds diehards and Leo Durocher will assure them that it is true.

18

KING ALOYSIUS

Al Simmons

"**I** HATE all pitchers," Al Simmons used to snarl. "Hits are my bread and butter. Pitchers are trying to take that bread and butter out of my mouth."

Pitchers didn't care much for Simmons, either. He was such a tremendous hitter that he was taking the bread and butter out of their mouths, too. The older Big Al got, the greedier he became for hits. He realized much too late that he would miss eligibility for the exclusive Three Thousand Hit Club and he went to his grave bitterly regretting it.

"Only seventy-six lousy hits," he would say. "That's all I needed. I made 2,924 hits in my career but I could kick myself for dogging it when I didn't have to. Many a time when I was young I'd ask Connie Mack to scratch my name off the lineup card when I was only a little bit off my feed or I'd take extra days off after an injury. If I'd had as much sense then as I do now, I could have had 3,000 hits—easy."

There are only eight men in the Three Thousand Hit Club and Simmons is in fancy company on the outside, including Babe Ruth, Lou Gehrig, Rogers Hornsby, Harry Heilmann, Tris Speaker, Ted Williams and so many great ones.

Yet Sim was so magnificent a ballplayer that he has been elected to the Hall of Fame. His lifetime average was .335, and twice he was the batting champion of the American League with marks of .381 and .390. But he also had two spectacular failures. One year he batted .386 and finished third (behind Heilmann's .393 and Speaker's .389) and two years later he batted .392 and finished second (behind Heilmann's .398).

He might have been unlucky in one other respect. When Simmons was a sandlot sensation in his hometown of Milwaukee, he spurned the offers of the Milwaukee Brewers. He wanted to play for John McGraw's Giants. So he wrote to Roger Bresnahan, who was running the Giant top farm team in Toledo. Large Aloysius merely asked for $150 carfare. It was refused.

So Milwaukee got him after all and sold him to the Philadelphia Athletics of Connie Mack. But the might-have-been kept haunting the thoughts of Simmons in the later years of his life.

"If Bresnahan had sent me the $150," he would remark wistfully, "it might have changed the course of baseball history. Can you imagine a right-handed power hitter like me in the Polo Grounds? I'd have given Babe Ruth's home run record of sixty a pretty good riffle."

As great a hitter as Simmons was, however, he was probably the most unorthodox batsman ever to make good in the big time. He committed the unpardonable sin of swinging "with his foot in the bucket." This meant that his front foot did not step ahead toward the pitcher when he strode into the ball but stabbed out toward third base. This style is used only by timid boys and by grown men who are terrified by curve balls. Big-leaguers? Never.

Never? Well, hardly ever. Simmons was the exception and he was afraid of nothing. No pitcher could scare him and he was a demon in the clutch. Old Connie figured out at the end of the 1930 season that Simmons had clouted fourteen homers in the eighth or ninth inning, each of which had a distinct bearing on the outcome of the game.

So the ancient Mr. Mack, who guarded his money with supreme care, gave Al a three-year contract for $100,000. To that Sim added endorsements and whatnot so that he earned $42,500 one season.

"And that cost me only $4,000 in income tax," added Al cheerfully. He was a big, bluff, hearty man with an intense will to win.

During those great years from 1929 to 1931 the Athletics had one of the most magnificent ball clubs ever assembled. Simmons was the clean-up hitter, flanked in the batting order by Mickey Cochrane and Jimmy Foxx.

This was the ball club which achieved one of the most stupendous rallies in World Series history, the never-to-be-forgotten fourth game in 1929 against the Cubs. Simmons —his original name was Szymanski—was the first batter in the memorable seventh inning, with the Cubs coasting along with an 8–0 lead. He hit a home run—and was mad.

"You dumb Polack," he growled to himself as he angrily flung away his bat. "Why do you waste home runs in a game like this?"

That made the score 8 to 1. But by the time Al came to bat again in the same inning, things had happened. The Athletics were only behind by a run, 8 to 7. Simmons just missed a second homer, the ball curving past the foul pole by inches. So he ripped off a single that tied the score and later scored himself in a totally unbelievable 10-run inning. Oh, yes. The A's won, 10 to 8.

Sim was remarkable when the stakes were down. When the swashbuckling Athletics were heading for another pennant in 1930, they came face to face with the Senators in a doubleheader of a crucial series. Washington led into the ninth inning of the first game, 6 to 3. Up stepped Big Al with a three-run homer to tie the score. The A's won eventu-

ally in the fifteenth, but not before Simmons had ruptured
a blood vessel in his leg with a slide into third.

They carted him to the clubhouse for repairs and the
examining physician sadly offered his diagnosis to ancient
Connie.

"Mr. Mack," he said, "Simmons won't be able to play
in the second game today. If you need him badly enough,
you can use him as a pinch hitter. But he had better hit
the ball into the stands because he can't run."

The doctor laughed hollowly at his little joke. So Al sat
on the bench, squirming in frustration because the Senators
had broken away to a 7–3 lead. In the ninth inning, however, the Athletics launched a promising rally by filling the
bases. With a long, bony finger Connie beckoned to
Simmons.

"By golly, Al," he chirped, "here's the spot to see if
that doctor knew what he was talking about. Go up there
and hit."

Did he hit? He slammed the first pitch into the stands
for a grand-slam homer. Happily he hobbled around the
bases as Connie beamed.

"Goodness gracious, Al," said the mild-mannered old
gentleman, "that was a nice one."

It tied the score and the A's jammed another run across
the plate to win the game, thereby planting their feet firmly
on Pennant Road.

They called him the Duke of Milwaukee and Al was
proud of his nickname. In fact, he was proud of virtually
every phase of his baseball career.

The Athletics trained at Fort Myers in Florida when Sim
was a young ballplayer, and that resort's most famous winter
resident was Thomas Alva Edison. Brilliant though Edison
was as an inventor, he was abysmally ignorant of baseball.

So the questions he asked Big Al when Connie introduced them were a mite startling.

"I'm pleased to meet you, Mr. Simmons," said Edison. "What position do you play? Are you a batter or a fielder?"

"I'm both, Mr. Edison," said Al proudly.

That he was. Not only was he a great hitter, he was a superlative outfielder as well. The finest tribute he ever received came from the stern Marse Joe McCarthy of the Yankees, a man sparing in his praise. It was given, more or less by accident, when the manager of the Bronx Bombers decided to switch the scatter-armed Blazin' Ben Chapman from third base to left field.

"I could tell you a lot about how to play that position," said McCarthy to Chapman, "but the best advice I can give you is to watch Al Simmons. Watch how he fields base hits, always in front of the ball and always in position to throw as soon as he gets his hands on it. Watch how fast he gets the ball away and how accurately he throws. Just try to be like him because he's the best left fielder I ever saw."

When Simmons first joined the Athletics, the coaching staff was horrified by his foot-in-the-bucket stance and wanted to change him to orthodoxy. Wise Connie put a stop to it fast.

"Leave him alone," ordered the old gentleman. "He must be a pretty good hitter. He batted .398 in the American Association last year and anyone who can hit like that can stand on his head at the plate for all I care."

When he first came up, pitchers jumped to wrong conclusions. They thought he was a scaredy-cat. They threw at his head. Down he'd go and arise white-faced. He wasn't white with fear. He was white with rage.

"Here comes one at your head, you yellow busher," taunted a pitcher one day.

"Just try it," said the grim-lipped Simmons.

He ducked away and sliced a home run into the right-field seats. Yankee pitchers rode him unmercifully in one series. Big Al came out of the series with eleven hits, ten for extra bases.

"I studied movies of myself," he was to say in his later years, "and I discovered that my left foot may have stabbed toward third base but the rest of me was in a proper line at the plate. My swing was level and I could hit with power."

World War II and the shortage of manpower extended the Simmons career quite a few years beyond its normal span. He didn't need the money. He hung on, even when he was fat and forty, because of his insatiable appetite for those extra base hits which would move him into the Three Thousand Hit Club. He'd sit wistfully on the bench, hoping that he'd get the call to pinch-hit.

Simmons slammed 307 home runs during a career which brought him fame, fortune and a place in the Hall of Fame. But he'd willingly have traded in every one of them for the seventy-six hits which would have given him 3,000.

19

KING ROGERS

"The Rajah," Rogers Hornsby

THE kid was a good fielder, all right. Bob Connery, scout for the St. Louis Cardinals, conceded that much. But so hopeless was the boy as a hitter that Connery hesitated. Yet the Cardinals of 1915 were so desperate for ballplayers that they were in no position to be fussy. Besides, the Dennison club of the old Western Association was only asking $500 for the nineteen-year-old Texan. The Cards bought him.

Thus did Rogers Hornsby sneak into the big leagues in the most ironic fashion of all—on the passport of his glove instead of his bat. What makes it seem so ridiculous in retrospect is that the Rajah was to become the greatest right-handed batsman who ever lived. His lifetime average for twenty-three seasons was to be a dazzling .358, a mark surpassed only by Ty Cobb's .367.

There was one absolutely incredible five-year span, though, that not even Cobb could match. During that stretch Hornsby *averaged* .402. Starting in 1921 he ripped off in succession—brace yourself for this!—marks of .397, .401, .384, .424 and .403. Seven times in all he was the batting champion of the National League.

The Rajah was a hitter without a weakness. He stood in the back corner of the batting box, as far from the plate as was legally possible. But he strode in with a beautiful level swing and could even murder the outside pitches to which he might have seemed vulnerable. He just waited, those steely blue eyes watching the pitcher with a gimlet-like stare.

The pitching fraternity tried everything to stop him, fast balls and curves, inside and outside, high and low. Nothing worked. One day a manager decided to try terror. A cold-blooded, strong-armed rookie was elected to start the game and fire beanballs at Hornsby to try to loosen him up. The Rajah stepped up to bat.

The kid threw a whistling fast ball at his head. Down went Hornsby into the dust. He arose, brushed himself off and uttered no complaint. In came another duster and another. Three times he went down and on each occasion he said not a word.

The umpire looked at his indicator which showed three balls and no strikes. The Rajah looked at the pitcher, eyes baleful and lips curling in contempt. At last he spoke.

"Okay, wise guy," he snarled, "whatcha gonna do now?"

The kid had to come in with a strike. Hornsby hit the ball out of the park.

Not long ago Hornsby was encountered. He has changed little. His hair is gray but his eyes are still steely blue, his square-jawed face florid and his figure still trim at 200 pounds on a frame a shade under six feet in height. He got to talking about homers and made a statement uncharacteristic of him.

"I wasn't much of a home run hitter," he said.

Oh, no? He was twice home run king of the National League with forty-two in 1922 and with thirty-nine in 1925. His lifetime total was 302, thereby making him eligible for the exclusive Three Hundred Club.

Ordinarily the outspoken Hornsby never has been known to say an unkind word about Hornsby. He has no false modesty. He was great and he was fully aware of it. Once I asked him what system he used to get out of a slump.

"When a man has a lifetime average of .358," he snapped, making his questioner feel like a dope, "he doesn't get into a slump. I doubt that I ever went two or three successive games without a hit."

The Rajah's outspokenness and bluntness endeared him to reporters because he never dodged a question. But his frankness continually got him in trouble with his employers and other ballplayers.

Branch Rickey was the manager of the Cardinals in 1923, 1924 and halfway through the 1925 season. It is probable that no man ever knew more baseball than the Mahatma. He made a science of it. But ballplayers of that era couldn't understand science and Rickey's fancy theories and fancy words were going over their heads. Finally Sam Breadon, the owner of the Redbirds, kicked the Mahatma upstairs where his genius had a better chance to flower. He made Rickey, the theoretician, his general manager and appointed the hard-boiled, practical Hornsby as his field manager.

The Rajah stalked into the clubhouse and pointed disdainfully to Rickey's blackboards, charts and graphs.

"Let's cut out this baloney," he said, "and just play ball."

The Cardinals did precisely that. They began their pickup immediately and in the following season of 1926 they won the first pennant in St. Louis history. On the way to the championship, however, the Rajah stomped on the boss's toes. Breadon, eager to make money, booked an exhibition game on an open date. Hornsby thought his wearied heroes were entitled to a rest and angrily bawled out Breadon, calling him a cheapskate. This episode opened a breach between them.

The Rajah was not interested in protecting his players as human beings but as a winning machine. He was coldly unsympathetic during his many managerial flings. He refused to congratulate a player for hitting a home run or for making a saving catch or pitching a low-hit game.

"Why should I?" he asked in his brusque fashion. "That's what they're being paid to do, isn't it?"

Technically he was correct but that lack of warmth prevented him from achieving the same mark as a manager which he had as a player.

After the Cardinals had won the World Series, he spoke his mind to Breadon and Sam reached the reluctant decision that he would have to unload his hot potato, then the biggest hero St. Louis ever had.

At the same time John McGraw of the Giants was having difficulties with a hot potato of his own, Frank Frisch, his captain and a second baseman. So they engineered a trade, one that rocked the baseball world, Hornsby for Frisch.

McGraw had the Rajah for a season and shipped him off to Boston. Two such outspoken men never could get along. Nor did Hornsby endear himself to the Giants when the Little Napoleon appointed him acting manager for a brief stretch during an illness.

One day Hornsby snarled at Freddie Lindstrom, a youthful firebrand, for not making a play the way he wanted it made.

"But the Old Man," said Freddie, "always told me to make it the way I did."

"When I'm running this ball club," said the Rajah coldly, "you'll do things the way I say."

Lindstrom exploded. "Who do you think you are?" screamed Lindy. "Once you put down your bat you're a detriment to the ball club."

Hornsby was traded to Boston and soon replaced Jack Slattery as manager. He eventually was shipped to the Cubs where he replaced Marse Joe McCarthy as manager. In the twilight of his playing career he managed the Browns. Then he wandered about the minors before another fling with the Browns, and lastly the Cincinnati Reds.

But if the undiplomatic Rajah couldn't manage, he certainly could play ball. Lindstrom's charge was a bit unfair because Hornsby was a fine second baseman and his only weakness was his total inability to catch pop flies.

At bat he had no weaknesses. One day in the Cincinnati clubhouse the pitchers were discussing Hornsby, and the one they questioned most was Jake May, the stocky little left-hander, who had faced him the day before.

"What did you throw him, Jake?" someone asked. "Have you any ideas?"

"I guess I tried everything," sighed Jake. "I gave him my high, hard one on the outside and he belted it for a homer. I gave him a change of pace and he hit a triple. I curved him and he got a double. I threw him chest high and he singled. I threw him knee high and he tripled again. The only safe thing is to roll the ball up to the plate."

If Hornsby claimed that he wasn't a homer hitter, he meant that he never went deliberately after one. The 302 he got were, so to speak, accidental. He met the ball where it was pitched and slammed ferocious line drives. Any one that got high enough had enough power to sail over the fence.

Line drives? Hornsby hit the wickedest line drives of all. One day Art Nehf fired one in and Hornsby hit back a line drive that caromed off his chest. The oddest part about this was that the A. G. Spalding label on the ball was stenciled on his skin for a week.

Other ballplayers were fully aware of the way the Rajah

sprayed his hits, depending on how they were pitched. A rookie wandered over to Jacques Fournier, the quaint Dodger first baseman, just before facing Hornsby.

"How do I pitch to this guy?" he asked.

"Just feed him inside pitches," said Jacques.

The Rajah almost decapitated the third baseman with a line drive.

"I thought you said inside pitches were his weakness," said the puzzled kid to Fournier.

"I said nothing of the kind," retorted M'sieu Jacques. "I just didn't want him hitting outside pitches on a line toward me. After all, I'm a married man with a family."

Few ballplayers were more dedicated than this lonesome man who took no part in the frivolity that makes a ball-player's life more bearable. Hornsby was a "loner"; he didn't mix in much with his mates. He never drank; he never smoked. So careful was he of protecting his keen eyesight that he wouldn't even go to the movies, the main off-the-field occupation of all ballplayers. He wouldn't even read the newspapers except for a fleeting glance at batting averages.

That's how he happened to become aware of the progress of Andy Cohen. When McGraw traded Hornsby to Boston, his idea was to install Cohen at second base and thereby realize one of his fondest dreams, a Jewish ballplayer as a Giant regular.

For a few weeks it looked to be a highly successful experiment. The likable and popular Cohen got off to such a successful start that one of the newspapers began to print a daily comparison box. "Cohen got three hits and is now batting .457. Hornsby went hitless and is batting .172." That went on for weeks. The Braves came to New York and the Rajah had a chance to speak his mind to his friends among the baseball writers.

"It's a dirty trick the papers are playing on that kid," he said. "Pretty soon I'll start to hit and then I'll leave Cohen so far behind that I'll lose him."

He was right, of course. Cohen did well with .274. But Hornsby set a Boston record with .387.

Like all great hitters, the Rajah brought a keen eye to the plate. He was so perceptive a judge of balls and strikes that the pitchers leveled the same complaint of him they level at all true artists with a bat, from Willie Keeler to Ted Williams. The umpires permit the eagle-eyed hitting wonders "to umpire their own games." The theory is that on close calls, the Boys in Blue defer to the judgment of the expert with the bat.

One afternoon Jumbo Jim Elliott of the Cubs whisked across two strikes on Hornsby. Then the king-sized pitcher fired in one that seemed to have caught a corner of the plate.

"Ball one," intoned Umpire Cy Pfirman.

Jumbo Jim promptly blew a fuse.

"You blind so-and-so," he howled. "It was a third strike."

Pfirman strode majestically toward the mound and bestowed a scathing glance in the direction of the big pitcher.

"Whenever it's a strike," he said, "Mr. Hornsby will let you know about it."

Elliott was so mad that he burned the next one over the middle with every ounce of strength at his command. Hornsby hit it over the fence for a home run.

In one respect the Rajah was the most remarkable of all the upper echelon of home run hitters because he took a prodigious share of singles, doubles and triples as well. His lifetime average of .358 is ample testimony of that.

He was all baseball, though. And there was nothing diplomatic about him—especially when he had a bat in his hands.

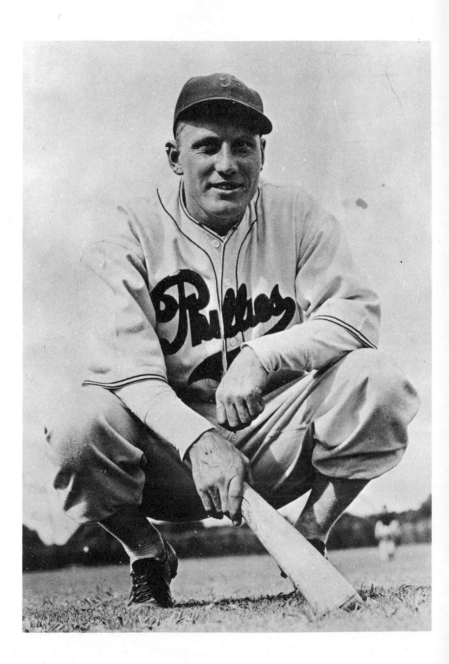

20

KING CHARLES

Chuck Klein

O F all the Kings of the Home Run the man least remembered is Charles (Chuck) Klein of the Philadelphia Phils, those paragons of futility. The big fellow barely qualified for regal accreditation, slipping past the line which separates baseball royalty from the peasants. He hit 300 home runs in his career.

He strolled into the Phillie clubhouse for the first time in July of 1928, a suitcase in each hand, and reported to the manager, Barney Shotton.

"I'm Klein," he said. "They call me Chuck Klein."

"All right, Klein," said the brusque Shotton. "Get into uniform. They tell me you can hit. Goodness knows, we need hitters." Suddenly a new thought struck him. Sadly he added, "We need everything." It was the understatement of the century.

The Phillies were the perennial doormats, a solid last-place team from opening day to the final game, year after year. Among their many handicaps was their ball park, Baker Bowl. This midget monstrosity was so small that pitchers felt as though they were operating in a suitcase. All afternoon long they would hear the clank of baseballs caroming off the tin fences. It was a gruesome sound.

Philadelphia pitchers wore out before their time. Games in Baker Bowl would be won by such tidy counts as 16 to 15, and there was one 1922 game when the Cubs defeated the Phils, 26 to 23. It was obviously quite a ball park, a hitter's delight.

In fact, the Phillies of 1930 compiled a team batting average of .315—and finished last. This raised many an eyebrow.

"How can you finish last with such a hitting club?" someone asked Shotton.

"Have you seen my pitching?" answered the coach with a wry grin.

The hitting was an interesting phenomenon, at that. Klein led the club that 1930 season with .386. Naturally enough, that got him nowhere because Bill Terry was ahead of him with .401 and so was Babe Herman with .393. But the Phils also had Lefty O'Doul .383, Pinky Whitney .342, Barney Friberg .341 and four other .300 batsmen.

The day Chuck reported he was used as a pinch hitter. He popped up. But the next day he started and slammed out the first of his 300 home runs. There is no question about the fact that Baker Bowl helped in their production, because Klein had successive years of 43, 40, 31, 38 and 28 before he was traded to the Cubs. Then both his batting average and homer output tailed off, both to perk up after his return to the Phils after two years' absence.

The jesters of Chuck's heyday said that Philadelphia newspapers used to keep the same headline in type: PHILS LOSE AS KLEIN HITS ANOTHER HOMER. That headline was in constant use.

The burly outfielder resented cracks to the effect that he was "a Baker Bowl hitter."

"Yes," he would admit with a frown, "I popped a few over the wall at Baker Bowl but I also slammed a lot of drives off that tin fence, drives that would have been homers in bigger parks.

"Where did I hit my four homers in one game? It was in

Forbes Field, one of the roomiest parks in the majors. And all four went into the seats high up."

That last one was the most convincing argument. The four-in-a-game feat put Klein in rather exclusive company and marks his closest approach to any sort of immortality. But he was awfully lucky to get the chance. In fact, he was twice lucky.

The Phils and Pirates were locked in a tight one. The Phils even would regard it as a low-scoring game. They were tied at the end of the ninth, 6 to 6. Thrice had Chuck hit homers that afternoon but a storm threatened to break before he ever would get a chance to come to bat in the tenth. But he made it, his fourth homer. Then he had to sweat it out while the Pirates got their last licks. Otherwise the score would have reverted to the nine-inning tie and Chuck's homer would have been washed out.

He was phenomenally strong and swung a 42-ounce bat in Babe Ruth fashion. But he had earned that strength. On summer vacations from Southport High in Indianapolis, he worked on a road gang, swinging a 24-pound sledgehammer. Later he had a job in a steel mill, tossing 200-pound ingots into a smelting furnace.

There was a slightly synthetic textile to his royal robes because they bore the label "Made in Baker Bowl." Yet Chuck Klein, the least ranking king, achieved something that the No. 1 king, Babe Ruth, never accomplished. The record books will forever show that on July 10, 1936, the Phillie slugger hit four home runs in one game.

Chuck also is the only player in history involved in a multi-player trade which saw him sold to the Cubs for $65,000 and which saw the Cubs give another $50,000 to the Phillies to take him back. This is the epitome of high finance.

21

KING ROGER

Roger Maris

B<small>Y</small> the middle of the 1961 season Roger Maris was hitting home runs at a pace far ahead of Babe Ruth's classic record of sixty homers in a 154-game campaign. Pretense was easy then. He was able to convince both himself and interviewers that he never gave the Babe's record a thought.

"Look," he said. "I swing hard. Sometimes the ball drops in and sometimes it doesn't. If I ever start worrying about it, I won't be worth a hill of beans."

By mid-September all pretense had fled. The ordeal of Roger Maris was etched on his face. There were dark circles under his troubled green eyes. His cheeks seemed sunken. And when he ran a comb through his darkish blond crew cut, clumps of hair came off on the comb from just above the nape of his neck. Anxiously, he went to the doctor.

"What causes it, doc?" he asked.

"Nervous tension," said the medical man.

Maris was in the grip of a vise, a vise that kept grinding a little closer every day. And an entire nation watched him squirm in torment under the pitiless glare of a publicity spotlight that burned into him with a fiercer intensity than into anyone else in sports history.

The sports gods of yesteryear—Babe Ruth, Jack Dempsey, Bobby Jones and the like—were subjected to a considerable amount of questioning by sportswriters. But it was casual and friendly. However, Maris had to undergo a Grand Inquisition day after endless day.

He was asked questions by writers he knew and by total strangers. He was pounced upon by television men, radio broadcasters and magazine chroniclers. He was asked penetrating questions that probed his secret thoughts and he was asked irritating, stupid questions, some of an insultingly personal nature. The fans gave him no peace. They hounded him wherever he went, including church.

"They even asked for my autograph at Mass," he said disgustedly.

Nor were all fans well-wishers. Some reviled him from the safety of the right-field stands or from the outer fringes of the crowds he drew with every step. They denounced him for trying to commit the sacrilege of breaking the Babe's record. They invaded his privacy with a rudeness, boorishness and lack of consideration that kept him in an angry whirl.

Under the circumstances it's remarkable that Roger performed as well as he did. He had heard from Hank Greenberg and from Jimmy Foxx about the tremendous pressures which start to crush down on anyone challenging the Babe's ghost. Never could he have dreamed that it would be as bad as it was. In fact, these were far more cruel than the pressures which had confronted them.

What made it all the more agonizing was that Maris was totally unprepared for his ordeal. Virtually overnight he was catapulted from the obscurity of being a journeyman ballplayer into the most talked-about man in the United States. Here was a chap who was boldly taking dead aim at one of baseball's most glamorous records. Who was he anyway?

Roger Eugene Maris was born on September 10, 1934, in Hibbing, Minnesota, the second son of a railroad man,

Rudolf. A dozen years later the family settled down in Fargo, North Dakota. Even as a small boy Roger loved the great outdoors and the only sport that appealed to him was hockey. Baseball interested him not a whit.

However, it did interest his older brother, Rudy. Not only was Rudy just as strong-willed, hotheaded and stubborn as Roger but he was bigger and stronger. Those last attributes came in handy whenever big brother went off to play baseball. He dragged kid brother with him. By the time they both were in Shanley Catholic High School in Fargo, little brother didn't have to be dragged to any athletic competition. He went of his own volition.

Shanley had no baseball team but it did have a football team. Roger became a standout halfback and by his senior year he was the leading scorer in the state. Scholarship offers came pouring in from colleges all over the country. When they began to come in, Roger was playing American Legion baseball and proving adept at it.

He weakened to the extent of going to the University of Oklahoma for an inspection tour. Coach Bud Wilkinson even persuaded him to take the entrance examination. Roger sat in the classroom, the paper in front of him and his eyes wandering to the great outdoors beyond the window. In dispirited fashion he answered a few questions on the test paper and stared out the window.

"This isn't for me," he said. He walked out.

The Cleveland Indians were interested in him. He went to the lake city, slammed a few baseballs for Hank Greenberg, then the general manager, and left with a message.

"Have your father phone me as soon as you get home," said the impressed Greenberg.

By then, however, the Cubs also were on his trail. He went to Wrigley Field in Chicago for a tryout.

"Go home," said the less perceptive Cubs. "You're too small. You'll never make it."

Actually there is nothing small about Maris. He's a 197-pound six-footer who doesn't look it. His build is compact and symmetrical. In street clothes or baseball uniform he seems ordinary in size—or less. But when he's sitting in front of his locker in the Yankee Stadium clubhouse, a truer appreciation of his physique instantly hits the eye. His upper arms and shoulders are heavily muscled. In the vernacular of the trade, "he strips big."

The man who first took cognizance of his size and converted him into a home run hitter was Jo-Jo White, the old Detroit outfielder. But that is jumping ahead of the story.

In March of 1953 the eighteen-year-old Maris went to the Cleveland minor league camp at Daytona Beach. He had received $5,000 for signing and the promise of another $10,000 when, as and if he made the varsity. That's when baseball men discovered what a strong-minded and determined chap Maris was. Although just a kid, he already had begun to form his reputation as one of baseball's Angry Young Men. He flatly refused to accept an assignment to a Class D team. He insisted not only on Class C but also on Fargo, his hometown.

"We never let a boy play in his hometown," said Mike McNally, the farm director. "It subjects him to too much pressure in trying to make good."

"Not me," said Roger coolly. "I'm going to Fargo. That's definite. Now it's up to you to decide whether I go there just to live on my own or whether I go there to play ball for the Cleveland organization."

McNally surrendered. Maris was assigned to Fargo. He hit .325 but had only nine homers. The next spring Maris had to fight for his rights again, something he did well. He was not promoted but kept on the Fargo list.

"Move me up to Class B or I quit," said Roger at the end of a long and violent argument. So he was promoted to Keokuk in the Three-Eye League, Class B. That's when he met White, his new manager.

"You're too big to be a spray hitter," said Jo-Jo. "You must learn to make use of that strength and power. You've got to become a pull hitter."

He became a pull hitter, and in this faster league his average stayed up at .315 while his homer output leaped to thirty-two. After that he was promoted without first having to issue an ultimatum. For the 1955 season it was Tulsa, a Class AA team.

Instantly the strong-willed Roger clashed with his manager, Dutch Meyer. The Angry Young Man—the other ballplayers term him a "red-neck"—rarely attempts to hide his feelings. He is too honest and forthright for that. After an unhappy and unprofitable month, he asked the Cleveland front office to transfer him to Reading in the Eastern League where his old boss and friend Jo-Jo White was manager. The request was granted. He did well for the balance of the season, although he certainly was no sensation.

The Indians looked him over in spring training and shipped him to Indianapolis for the 1956 season. This brought no cheers from Maris. He felt he had been given too quick a brush-off by Manager Al Lopez. He brooded and started so badly that he was benched. But once he was returned to the lineup, he had a good year and finally seemed ready for the big time.

In fact he seemed so ready in the spring of 1957 that the experts picked him to be the rookie of the year. He wasn't. He began like one and was a solid .300-plus hitter. Slamming into second base to break up a double play, he broke a rib. Upon his return, he could not regain his earlier form. He finished with an average of .235 and fourteen homers.

This hardly indicated that here was a challenger to Babe Ruth's record.

A front office upheaval at the season's end brought in Frank Lane as the Cleveland general manager. The bustling, mercurial Frantic Frankie has never been lacking in ideas. One of his first was to give Maris a speed-up course in his baseball education.

"I want you to play winter ball," said the breezy Lane.

"Not me," said the forthright Roger. "I won't play winter ball. I've been away from my wife and family too long. I'm going home."

He did, of course. No one ever can push Maris around against his will. But he and Lane were hardly chummy from that point on. Minutes before the trading deadline in June of 1958, Trader Lane traded Roger to Kansas City. If that now smacks of being a stupid trade, it wasn't. Cleveland got two regulars, Vic Power and Woody Held, for him. Maris wound up with less than an ordinary year, a .240 average and twenty-eight homers.

In the next season he started sensationally but then was stricken by appendicitis. The touch had been lost upon his return to the lineup as he finished with .273 and sixteen homers. By the time the Yankees swung the trade for him that December, Maris was far richer in promise than in actual accomplishment.

Casey Stengel announced that Maris would be his left fielder and Roger winced. He always had been a right fielder but he had too much respect and awe for the Ol' Perfessor to make one of his customary blunt refusals.

"I'd rather play right," he said cautiously that spring, "but I'm willing to play wherever the manager thinks I'll help most."

All during the exhibition season Roger was stationed in left and performed with his usual competence. So the unpredictable Stengel placed him in his lineup on opening day as—you guessed it—his right fielder. The overjoyed Maris celebrated his debut as a Yankee with two homers, a double and a single.

He stayed hot, too. With Mantle physically below par and contributing little for the first half of the season, Maris carried the ball club on his broad shoulders. An injury in August nudged him out of the lineup but by that time Master Mickey had assumed the burden. Mantle carried the team in the last half.

One of them had to be the Most Valuable Player. But which? Was the first half by Maris more important than the second half by Mantle? The experts decided that it was. Roger won the MVP award by three points. But he didn't win the homer championship. Mickey's closing rush edged him out, forty to thirty-nine.

There wasn't the slightest hint in the early part of the 1961 season that the pair of them would be pursuing the Babe's ghost. Roger began wretchedly. He didn't hit his first homer until the tenth game. He went almost a week before he got his second. Three days later he got his third.

"The fourth was so long in coming," he said ruefully, "that I was beginning to wonder if I'd ever hit it." This one didn't arrive for another nine days. Roger was confused and troubled. He was invited to lunch with Dan Topping, co-owner of the Yankees, and Roy Hamey, the general manager.

"We're not paying you for a fancy average," said Hamey. "We're paying you to hit homers."

"Stop worrying," said Topping. "Swing for the fences. The average will take care of itself."

As later events were to prove, this was a most important pep talk. Roger put aside his anxieties and began to do what came naturally. He piled up the homers. But so did

Mantle. They were booming along at such a rate that the whole country awakened to this twin assault on the Ruthian mark as first one and then the other surged ahead or increased his total.

Magazine writers, not knowing the men and probing for angles that weren't there, tried to get either to admit that a jealous feud already had arisen.

"Listen," said Roger, angrily biting off the words. "I'm sharing an apartment with Bob Cerv and Mantle. We live together. And no one lives with someone he doesn't like."

By late August the free-swinging Maris had broken away from Mantle in their home run derby. It looked as though he couldn't possibly miss the Babe's record. But the Babe's ghost is mighty powerful. He even haunts in Ruthian style.

The pitchers began to prey on Roger's overeagerness, his obsession for homers. They fed him good pitches only by accident as they tantalized him with tosses off the target. Outside pressures mounted. No longer did he share interviewers with Mantle. He drew them all and there were ten times as many of them as had previously been the case. His innocent words were lifted from context until he sounded like a swell-headed churl. He was bewitched, bothered, bewildered.

On September 9 Roger hit his fifty-sixth homer. This gave him eleven days and twelve games for catching the Babe within the 154-game span. Then the Ruth hex seemed to take over. Hurricane Carla whirled her skirts and the fringes reached Chicago. Rain cut a game short. Winds blew against him in the next couple. In Detroit he was stopped until he tagged Frank Lary for No. 57. But the wheels had tightened on the rack which was torturing him. He was only four games away from the end.

Suddenly the Babe's ghost became careless. There's no other explanation. Roger had been shut out again against the Tigers. Then Moose Skowron made an error to permit the Bengals to tie the score. The reprieved Maris clouted No. 58 in the twelfth inning, an inning which never would have been played had not the error been committed.

By that time the pressures were almost unbearable. Roger came into the 154th game against the Orioles in Baltimore needing two homers to tie and three homers to break the magic mark.

"Not even Houdini could do it," said Roger in gaunt-eyed despair.

But he sure gave it a noble try. In an early inning off the artful Milt Pappas, Roger crashed out No. 59. It swept him past Greenberg and Foxx, the smiters of fifty-eight homers. Only the king himself had ever hit more.

By the time Maris stepped to bat for a final fling the knuckle-balling Hoyt Wilhelm was on the mound for the Orioles, the toughest pitcher of all in such a crisis.

"Here's your last chance, Rog," sympathetically said Gus Triandos, the Oriole catcher. "Think you have another good one left in your bat?"

"I hope so," said Maris. "Don't think my collar isn't tight."

The collar tight? The whole world seemed to be pressing down around him in a giant constriction that was squeezing the life out of him. He tried to wait for a good pitch. But even Wilhelm's good pitches flutter and dance and misbehave.

Roger saw a good one coming. He started to swing, saw it wasn't good after all and checked the swing. But in his anxiety he had committed himself too much. The ball hit the bat and trickled to the left of the mound. A bold bid was over.

He should have relaxed for the extra eight games of the expanded 162-game season. But that inner urgency never

left him. He still wanted what glory there would be in match-
ing or surpassing the Babe. It took him almost a week to
reach No. 60. It was in the 158th game. And then in the
final game of the year he blasted No. 61.

What did he think of as he was circling the bases after
that historic clout?

"Nothing," he said weariedly. "No one could believe that
a guy's mind could go blank at such a time. But mine was."

That feeling of shocked numbness was still with him in
the World Series. He was like a sleepwalker, a man in a
trance. He answered questions mechanically and dully. All
the life and sparkle was gone from him. He did hit one
homer in the rout of the Cincinnati Reds, even winning a
ball game with it. But most of the time he couldn't even
knock the ball out of the infield.

Either through coincidence or an ironic fate the Maris
homer output for regular season and post-season play was
sixty-two. This was identical with Ruth's 1927 total because
the Babe had slammed a pair in the World Series.

If Roger thought he was hearing voices in his semi-
comatose condition at the end, he could have been right.
One would have been the booming voice of the Babe roaring with a mocking laughter.

"Nice try, keed," he would have said. "The ol' Babe is
a tough one to catch, eh?"

He sure is. When Roger Maris hit his sixty-first home run,
it left him a mere 556 homers behind the Babe in lifetime
totals.

"I'm not trying to replace Babe Ruth," Maris kept insisting all season long.

He couldn't. No ballplayer ever could.

RECORDS OF THE KINGS

The lifetime records of
twenty kings of the
home run.

GEORGE HERMAN RUTH

Born, Feb. 6, 1895, at Baltimore, Md.
Height, 6:02. Weight, 220. Brown eyes and Mack hair.
Throw and batted left-handed

Year Club	League	G.	AB.	R.	H.	2B.	3B.	HR.	RBI.	B.A.
1914–Balt.-Prov. ....International		46	121	22	28	2	10	1	...	.231
1914–Boston ....American		5	10	1	2	1	0	0	0	.200
1915–Boston ....American		42	92	16	29	10	1	4	20	.315
1916–Boston ....American		67	136	18	37	5	3	3	16	.272
1917–Boston ....American		52	123	14	40	6	3	2	10	.325
1918–Boston ....American		95	317	50	95	26	11	11	64	.300
1919–Boston(a)............American		130	432	103	139	34	12	29	112	.322
1920–New York............American		142	458	158	172	36	9	54	137	.376
1921–New York............American		152	540	177	204	44	16	59	170	.378
1922–New York............American		110	406	94	128	24	8	25	96	.315
1923–New York..........American		152	522	151	205	45	13	41	130	.393
1924–New York............American		153	529	143	200	39	7	46	121	.378
1925–New York............American		98	359	61	104	12	2	35	66	.290
1926–New York ....American		152	495	139	184	30	5	47	155	.372
1927–New York............American		151	540	158	192	29	8	60	164	.356
1928–New York............American		154	536	163	173	29	8	54	142	.323
1929–New York............American		135	499	121	172	26	6	46	154	.345
1930–New York............American		145	518	150	186	28	9	49	153	.359
1931–New York............American		145	534	149	199	31	3	46	163	.373
1932–New York............American		133	457	120	156	13	5	41	137	.341
1933–New York............American		137	459	97	138	21	3	34	103	.301
1934–New York(b) ....American		125	365	78	105	17	4	22	84	.288
1935–Boston ....National		28	72	13	13	0	0	6	12	.181
Major League Totals...................		2503	8399	2174	2873	506	136	714	2209	.342

(a) Sold to New York A. L. for $125,000, January 3, 1920.
(b) Released to Boston Braves, February 26, 1935.

WORLD'S SERIES RECORD

Year Club	League	G.	AB.	R.	H.	2B.	3B.	HR.	RBI.	B.A.
1915–Boston ....American		1	1	0	0	0	0	0	0	.000
1916–Boston ....American		1	5	0	0	0	0	0	0	.200
1918–Boston ....American		3	5	0	1	0	1	0	2	.200
1921–New York............American		6	16	3	5	0	0	1	4	.313
1922–New York............American		5	17	1	2	1	0	0	1	.118
1923–New York............American		6	19	8	7	1	1	3	3	.368
1926–New York............American		7	20	6	6	0	0	4	5	.300
1927–New York............American		4	15	4	6	0	0	2	7	.400
1928–New York............American		4	16	9	10	3	0	3	4	.625
1932–New York............American		4	15	6	5	0	0	2	6	.333
World's Series Totals...................		41	129	37	42	5	2	15	32	.325

PITCHING RECORD

Year Club	League	G.	IP.	W.	L.	Pct.	H.	R.	ER.	BB.	SO.	ERA.
1914–Balt.-Prov. ....International		35	245	22	9	.709	210	88	..	101	139	
1914–Boston ....American		4	23	2	1	.667	21	12	10	7	3	3.91
1915–Boston ....American		32	218	18	8	.692	166	80	59	85	112	2.44
1916–Boston ....American		44	324	23	12	.657	230	83	63	118	170	1.75
1917–Boston ....American		41	326	24	13	.649	244	93	73	108	128	2.02
1918–Boston ....American		20	166	13	7	.650	125	51	41	49	40	2.22
1919–Boston ....American		17	133	9	5	.643	148	59	44	58	30	2.97
1920–New York............American		1	4	1	0	1.000	3	4	2	2	0	4.50
1921–New York............American		2	9	2	0	1.000	14	10	9	9	2	9.00
1930–New York............American		1	9	1	0	1.000	11	3	3	3	2	3.00
1933–New York............American		1	9	1	0	1.000	12	5	5	3	0	5.00
Major League Totals...................		163	1221	94	46	.671	974	400	309	442	487	2.28

WORLD'S SERIES PITCHING RECORD

Year Club	League	G.	IP.	W.	L.	Pct.	H.	R.	ER.	BB.	SO.	ERA.
1916–Boston ....American		1	14	1	0	1.000	6	1	1	3	4	0.64
1918–Boston ....American		2	17	2	0	1.000	13	2	2	7	4	1.06
World's Series Totals ....;		3	31	3	0	1.000	19	3	3	10	8	0.87

JAMES EMORY FOXX

Born, Oct. 22, 1907, at Sudlersville, Md.

Height, 5:11 1/2. Weight, 200. Blue eyes and brown hair.

Threw and batted right-handed

Year.	Club.	League	G.	AB.	R.	H.	2B.	3B.	HR.	RBI.	B.A.
1924—Easton		East. Sh.	76	260	33	77	11	2	10	...	.296
1925—Philadelphia		American	10	9	2	6	1	0	0	0	.667
1925—Providence		International	41	101	12	33	6	3	1	15	.327
1926—Philadelphia		American	26	32	8	10	2	1	0	5	.313
1927—Philadelphia		American	61	130	23	42	6	5	3	20	.323
1928—Philadelphia		American	118	400	85	131	29	10	13	79	.328
1929—Philadelphia		American	149	517	123	183	23	9	33	117	.354
1930—Philadelphia		American	153	562	127	188	33	13	37	156	.335
1931—Philadelphia		American	139	515	93	150	32	10	30	120	.291
1932—Philadelphia		American	154	585	151	213	33	9	58	169	.364
1933—Philadelphia		American	149	573	125	204	37	9	48	163	.356
1934—Philadelphia		American	150	539	120	180	28	6	44	130	.334
1935—Philadelphia (a)		American	147	535	118	185	33	7	36	115	.346
1936—Boston		American	155	585	130	198	32	8	41	143	.338
1937—Boston		American	150	569	111	162	24	6	36	127	.285
1938—Boston		American	149	565	139	197	33	9	50	175	.349
1939—Boston		American	124	467	130	168	31	10	35	105	.360
1940—Boston		American	144	515	106	153	30	4	36	119	.297
1941—Boston		American	135	487	87	146	27	8	19	105	.300
1942—Boston (b)		American	30	100	18	27	4	0	5	14	.270
1942—Chicago		National	70	205	25	42	8	0	3	19	.205
1943—Chicago		National					(Did not play)				
1944—Chicago (c)		National	15	20	0	1	1	0	0	2	.050
1944—Portsmouth (d)		Pied.	5	2	0	0	0	0	0	0	.000
1945—Philadelphia		National	89	224	30	60	11	1	7	38	.268
1946—						(Out of Organized Ball)					
1947—St. Petersburg		Florida Int.	6	6	0	1	..	..	..	...	.167

Major League Totals 2317   8134   1751   2646   458   125   534   1921   .325

(a) Traded with Pitcher John Marcum to Boston Red Sox for Pitcher Gordon Rhodes, Catcher George Savino and $150,000, December 10, 1935.

(b) Released on waivers to Chicago Cubs, June 1, 1942.

(c) Released as player and signed as coach, July 6, 1944; released to Portsmouth as manager, August 25, 1944.

(d) Released by Portsmouth, December, 1944, and signed by Philadelphia Phillies, February 10, 1945.

WORLD'S SERIES RECORD

Year.	Club.	League	G.	AB.	R.	H.	2B.	3B.	HR.	RBI.	B.A.
1929—Philadelphia		American	5	20	5	7	1	0	2	5	.350
1930—Philadelphia		American	6	21	3	7	2	1	1	3	.348
1931—Philadelphia		American	7	23	3	8	0	0	1	3	.348
World's Series Totals			18	64	11	22	3	1	4	11	.344

THEODORE SAMUEL WILLIAMS

Born, Aug. 30, 1918, at San Diego, Calif.
Height, 6:04. Weight, 210. Greenish-brown eyes and brown hair,
Threw right and batted left-handed

Year.	Club.	League.	Pos.	G.	AB.	R.	H.	2B.	3B.	HR.	RBI.	B.A.	PO.
1936—San Diego		P. C.	OF	42	107	18	29	8	2	0	11	.271	64
1937—San Diego		P. C.	OF	138	454	66	132	24	2	23	98	.291	213
1938—Minneapolis		A. A.	OF	148	528	130	193	30	9	43	142	.366	269
1939—Boston		American	OF	149	565	131	185	44	11	31	145	.327	318
1940—Boston		American	OF-P	144	561	134	193	43	14	23	113	.344	302
1941—Boston		American	OF	143	456	135	185	33	3	37	120	.406	262
1942—Boston		American	OF	150	522	141	186	34	5	36	137	.356	313
1943-44-45—Boston		American					(In Military Service)						
1946—Boston		American	OF	150	514	142	176	37	8	38	123	.342	325
1947—Boston		American	OF	156	528	125	181	40	9	32	114	.343	347
1948—Boston		American	OF	137	509	124	188	44	3	25	127	.369	289
1949—Boston		American	OF	155	566	150	194	39	3	43	159	.343	337
1950—Boston (a)		American	OF	89	334	82	106	24	1	28	97	.317	165
1951—Boston		American	OF	148	531	109	169	28	4	30	126	.318	315
1952—Boston (b)		American	OF	6	10	2	4	0	1	1	3	.400	4
1953—Boston (b)		American	OF	37	91	17	37	6	0	13	34	.407	31
1954—Boston		American	OF	117	386	93	133	23	1	29	89	.345	213
1955—Boston		American	OF	98	320	77	114	21	3	28	83	.356	170
1956—Boston		American	OF	136	400	71	138	28	2	24	82	.345	174
1957—Boston		American	OF	132	420	96	163	28	1	38	87	.388	215
1958—Boston		American	OF	129	411	81	135	23	2	26	85	.328	154
1959—Boston		American	OF	103	272	32	69	15	0	10	43	.254	94
1960—Boston		American	OF	113	310	56	98	15	0	29	72	.316	131

Major League Totals .... 2292 7706 1798 1654 525 71 521 1839 .344 4159

(a) Suffered fractured left elbow when he crashed into the left-field wall making catch in first inning of All-Star Game at Chicago, July 11, 1950; despite injury he stayed in game until ninth inning. Williams had played 70 American League games up to the All-Star affair—but appeared in only 19 more contests with the Red Sox for the rest of the season.

(b) In Military Service most of the season.

PITCHING RECORD

Year.	Club.	League.	G.	IP.	W.	L.	Pct.	H.	R.	ER.	SO.	BB.	Ave.
1940—Boston		American	1	2	0	0	.000	3	1	1	1	0	4.50

WORLD'S SERIES RECORD

Year.	Club.	League.	Pos.	G.	AB.	R.	H.	2B.	3B.	HR.	RBI.	B.A.
1946—Boston		American	OF	7	25	2	5	0	0	0	1	.200

ALL-STAR GAME RECORD

Year.	League.	Pos.	AB.	R.	H.	2B.	3B.	HR.	RBI.	B.A.
1940—American		OF	2	0	0	0	0	0	0	.000
1941—American		OF	4	1	2	1	0	1	4	.500
1942—American		OF	4	0	1	0	0	0	0	.250
1946—American		OF	4	4	4	0	0	2	5	1.000
1947—American		OF	4	0	2	1	0	0	0	.500
1948—American		PH	0	0	0	0	0	0	0	.000
1949—American		OF	2	1	0	0	0	0	0	.000
1950—American		OF	4	0	1	0	0	0	1	.250
1951—American		OF	3	0	1	0	1	0	0	.333
1954—American		OF	2	1	0	0	0	0	0	.000
1955—American		OF	3	1	1	0	0	0	0	.333
1956—American		OF	4	1	1	0	0	1	2	.250
1957—American		Of	3	1	0	0	0	0	0	.000
1958—American		OF	2	0	0	0	0	0	0	.000
1959—American (both games)		PH-OF	3	0	0	0	0	0	0	.000
1960—American (both games)		PH	2	0	1	0	0	0	0	.500

All-Star Game Totals .... 46 10 14 2 1 4 12 .304

MELVIN THOMAS OTT

Born, March 2, 1909, at Gretna, La.

Height, 5:09. Weight, 170. Brown eyes and hair.

Threw right and batted left-handed

Year.	Club.	League.	Pos.	G.	AB.	R.	H.	2B.	3B.	HR.	RBI.	B.A.
1926—New York		National	OF	35	60	7	23	2	0	0	4	.383
1927—New York		National	OF	82	163	23	46	7	3	1	19	.282
1928—New York		National	OF	124	435	69	140	26	4	18	77	.322
1929—New York		National	OF	150	545	138	179	37	2	42	151	.328
1930—New York		National	OF	148	521	122	182	34	5	25	119	.349
1931—New York		National	OF	138	497	104	145	23	8	29	115	.292
1932—New York		National	OF	154	566	119	180	30	8	38	123	.318
1933—New York		National	OF	152	580	98	164	36	1	23	103	.283
1934—New York		National	OF	153	582	119	190	29	10	35	135	.326
1935—New York		National	OF-3B	152	593	113	191	33	6	31	114	.322
1936—New York		National	OF	150	534	120	175	28	6	33	135	.328
1937—New York		National	3B-OF	151	545	99	160	28	2	31	95	.294
1938—New York		National	3B-OF	150	527	116	164	23	6	36	116	.311
1939—New York		National	3B-OF	125	396	85	122	23	2	27	80	.308
1940—New York		National	OF-3B	151	536	89	155	27	3	19	79	.289
1941—New York		National	OF	148	525	89	150	29	0	27	90	.286
1942—New York		National	OF	152	549	118	162	21	0	30	93	.295
1943—New York		National	OF-3B	125	380	65	89	12	2	18	47	.234
1944—New York		National	OF-3B	120	399	91	115	16	4	20	82	.288
1945—New York		National	OF	135	451	73	139	23	0	21	79	.308
1946—New York		National	OF	31	68	2	5	1	0	1	4	.074

Major League Totals .... 2726 9452 1859 2876 488 72 511 1860 .304

WORLD'S SERIES RECORD

Year.	Club.	League.	Pos.	G.	AB.	R.	H.	2B.	3B.	HR.	RBI.	B.A.
1935—New York		National	OF	5	18	3	7	0	0	2	4	.389
1936—New York		National	OF	6	23	4	7	2	0	1	3	.304
1937—New York		National	3B	5	20	1	4	0	0	1	3	.200

World's Series Totals .... 16 61 8 18 2 0 4 10 .295

ALL-STAR GAME RECORD

Year.	League			Pos.	AB.	R.	H.	2B.	3B.	HR.	RBI.	B.A.
1934—National				OF	2	0	0	0	0	0	0	.000
1935—National				OF	4	0	0	0	0	0	0	.000
1936—National				PH-OF	1	0	1	0	0	0	0	1.000
1937—National				PH	1	0	1	1	0	0	0	1.000
1938—National				OF	4	1	1	0	1	0	0	.250
1939—National				OF	4	0	2	0	0	0	0	.500
1940—National				OF	0	1	0	0	0	0	0	.000
1941—National				PH	1	0	0	0	0	0	0	.000
1942—National				OF	4	0	0	0	0	0	0	.000
1943—National				PH	1	0	0	0	0	0	0	.000
1944—National				PH	1	0	0	0	0	0	0	.000

All-Star Game Totals .... 23 2 5 1 1 0 0 .217

HENRY LOUIS GEHRIG

Born, June 19, 1903, at New York, N.Y.

Height, 6:01. Weight, 212. Blue eyes and brown hair.

Threw and batted left-handed

Year.	Club.	League.	Pos.	G.	AB.	R.	H.	2B.	3B.	HR.	RBI.	B.A.
1921–Hartford		Eastern	1B	12	46	5	12	1	0	0	...	.261
1922–					(Not in Organized Ball)							
1923–New York		American	1B	13	26	6	11	4	1	1	9	.423
1923–Hartford		Eastern	1B	59	277	54	69	13	8	24	...	.304
1924–New York		American	Util	10	12	2	6	1	0	0	6	.500
1924–Hartford		Eastern	1B	134	504	111	186	40	13	37	...	.369
1925–New York		American	1B	126	437	73	129	23	9	21	68	.295
1926–New York		American	1B	155	572	135	179	47	20	16	107	.313
1927–New York		American	1B	155	584	149	218	52	18	47	175	.373
1928–New York		American	1B	154	562	139	210	47	13	27	142	.374
1929–New York		American	1B	154	553	127	166	33	9	35	126	.300
1930–New York		American	1B	154	581	143	220	42	17	41	174	.379
1931–New York		American	1B	155	619	163	211	31	15	46	184	.341
1932–New York		American	1B	156	596	138	208	42	9	34	151	.349
1933–New York		American	1B	152	593	138	198	41	12	32	139	.334
1934–New York		American	1B	154	579	128	210	40	6	49	165	.363
1935–New York		American	1B	149	535	125	176	25	10	30	119	.329
1936–New York		American	1B	155	579	167	205	37	7	49	152	.354
1937–New York		American	1B	157	569	138	200	37	9	37	159	.351
1938–New York		American	1B	157	576	115	170	32	6	29	114	.295
1939–New York		American	1B	8	28	2	4	0	0	0	1	.143
Major League Totals				2164	8001	1888	2721	535	161	494	1991	.340

Played under name of Lewis with Hartford in 1921.

WORLD'S SERIES RECORD

Year.	Club.	League.	Pos.	G.	AB.	R.	H.	2B.	3B.	HR.	RBI.	B.A.
1926–New York		American	1B	7	23	1	8	2	0	0	3	.348
1927–New York		American	1B	4	13	2	4	2	2	0	5	.308
1928–New York		American	1B	4	11	5	6	1	0	4	9	.545
1932–New York		American	1B	4	17	9	9	1	0	3	8	.529
1936–New York		American	1B	6	24	5	7	1	0	2	7	.292
1937–New York		American	1B	5	17	4	5	1	1	1	3	.294
1938–New York		American	1B	4	14	4	4	0	0	0	0	.286
World's Series Totals				34	119	30	43	8	3	10	35	.361

ALL-STAR GAME RECORD

Year.	League.	Pos.	AB.	R.	H.	2B.	3B.	HR.	RBI.	B.A.
1933–American		1B	2	0	0	0	0	0	0	.000
1934–American		1B	4	1	0	0	0	0	0	.000
1935–American		1B	3	1	0	0	0	0	0	.000
1936–American		1B	2	1	1	0	0	1	1	.500
1937–American		1B	4	1	2	1	0	1	4	.500
1938–American		1B	3	0	1	0	0	0	0	.333
All-Star Game Total			18	4	4	1	0	2	5	.222

STANLEY FRANK MUSIAL

Born, Nov. 21, 1920, at Donora, Pa.
Height, 6:00. Weight, 180. Brown eyes and hair.
Threw and batted left-handed

Year. Club.	League.	Pos.	G.	AB.	R.	H.	2B.	3B.	HR.	RBI.	B.A.
1938—Williamson	Mt. St.	P	26	62	5	16	3	0	1	6	.258
1939—Williamson	Mt. St.	P-PH	23	71	10	25	3	3	1	9	.352
1940—Daytona Beach	Fla. St.	OF-P	113	405	55	126	17	10	1	70	.311
1941—Springfield	W.A.	OF	87	348	100	132	27	10	26	94	.379
1941—Rochester	International	OF	54	221	43	72	10	4	3	21	.326
1941—St. Louis	National	OF	12	47	8	20	4	0	1	7	.426
1942—St. Louis	National	OF	140	467	87	147	32	10	10	72	.315
1943—St. Louis	National	OF	157	617	108	220	48	20	13	81	.357
1944—St. Louis	National	OF	146	568	112	197	51	14	12	94	.347
1945—St. Louis	National				(In Military Service)						
1946—St. Louis	National	1B-OF	156	624	124	228	50	20	16	103	.365
1947—St. Louis	National	1B	149	587	113	183	30	13	19	95	.312
1948—St. Louis	National	OF-1B	155	611	135	230	46	18	39	131	.376
1949—St. Louis	National	OF-1B	157	612	128	207	41	13	36	123	.338
1950—St. Louis	National	OF-1B	146	555	105	192	41	7	28	109	.346
1951—St. Louis	National	OF-1B	152	578	124	205	30	12	32	108	.355
1952—St. Louis	National	O-1B-P	154	578	105	194	42	6	21	91	.336
1953—St. Louis	National	OF	157	593	127	200	53	9	30	113	.337
1954—St. Louis	National	OF-1B	153	591	120	195	41	9	35	126	.330
1955—St. Louis	National	1B-OF	154	562	97	179	30	5	33	108	.319
1956—St. Louis	National	1B-OF	156	594	87	184	33	6	27	109	.310
1957—St. Louis	National	1B	134	502	82	176	38	3	29	102	.351
1958—St. Louis	National	1B	135	472	64	159	35	2	17	62	.337
1959—St. Louis	National	1B-OF	115	341	37	87	13	2	14	44	.255
1960—St. Louis	National	OF-1B	116	331	49	91	17	1	17	63	.275
1961—St. Louis	National	OF	123	372	46	107	22	4	15	70	.288
Major League Totals			2767	10,202	1858	3401	697	174	444	1811	.333

WORLD'S SERIES RECORD

Year. Club.	League.	Pos.	G.	AB.	R.	H.	2B.	3B.	HR.	RBI.	B.A.
1942—St. Louis	National	OF	5	18	2	4	1	0	0	2	.222
1943—St. Louis	National	OF	5	18	2	5	0	0	0	0	.278
1944—St. Louis	National	OF	6	23	2	7	2	0	1	2	.304
1946—St. Louis	National	1B	7	27	3	6	4	1	0	4	.222
World's Series Totals			23	86	9	22	7	1	1	8	.256

ALL-STAR GAME RECORD

Year. League	Pos.	AB.	R.	H.	2B.	3B.	HR.	RBI.	B.A.
1943—National	OF	4	0	1	1	0	0	1	.250
1944—National	OF	4	1	1	0	0	0	1	.250
1946—National	OF	2	0	0	0	0	0	0	.000
1947—National	PH	1	0	0	0	0	0	0	.000
1948—National	OF	4	1	2	0	0	1	2	.500
1949—National	OF	4	1	3	0	0	1	2	.750
1950—National	1B	5	0	0	0	0	0	0	.000
1951—National	OF	4	1	2	0	0	1	1	.500
1952—National	OF	2	1	0	0	0	0	0	.000
1953—National	OF	4	0	2	0	0	0	0	.500
1954—National	OF	5	1	2	0	0	0	0	.400
1955—National	OF	4	1	1	0	0	1	1	.250
1956—National	OF	4	1	1	0	0	1	1	.250
1957—National	1B	3	1	1	1	0	0	0	.333
1958—National	1B	4	1	1	0	0	0	0	.250
1959—National (both games)	PH-1B	1	0	0	0	0	0	0	.000
1960—National (both games)	PH	2	1	2	0	0	1	1	1.000
1961—National (both games)	PH	2	0	0	0	0	0	0	.000
All-Star Game Totals		59	11	19	2	0	6	10	.322

PITCHING RECORD

Year. Club.	League.	G.	IP.	W.	L.	Pct.	H.	R.	ER.	SO.	BB.	Ave.
1938—Williamson	Mt. State	20	110	6	6	.500	114	57	57	66	80	4.66
1939—Williamson	Mt. State	13	92	9	2	.818	71	53	44	86	85	4.30
1940—Daytona Beach	Fla. State	28	223	18	5	.783	179	108	65	176	145	2.62
1952—St. Louis (a)	National	1	0	0	0	.000	0	0	0	0	0	0.00
Major League Totals		1	0	0	0	.000	0	0	0	0	0	0.00

(a) Pitched to one batter, Frank Baumholtz of Chicago Cubs, as part of last-game-of-season stunt; Baumholtz, normally a left-handed hitter, switched to the right side of the plate and grounded first pitch to third baseman, who fumbled for an error.

EDWIN DONALD SNIDER

Born, Sept. 19, 1926, at Los Angeles, Calif.
Height, 6:00. Weight, 200. Blue eyes and brown hair.
Threw right and batted left-handed

Year.	Club.	League.	Pos.	G.	AB.	R.	H.	2B.	3B.	HR.	RBI.	B.A.
1944—Montreal	International	PH	2	2	0	0	0	0	0	0	0	.000
1944—Newport News	Piedmont	OF	131	507	87	149	34	6	9	50	.294
1945—Newport News	Piedmont		(In Military Service)									
1946—Fort Worth	Texas	OF	68	232	36	58	13	1	5	20	.250
1947—St. Paul	A. A.	OF	66	269	59	85	22	7	12	46	.316
1947—Brooklyn	National	OF	40	83	6	20	3	1	0	5	.241
1948—Montreal	International	OF	77	275	67	90	28	4	17	77	.327
1948—Brooklyn	National	OF	53	160	22	39	6	6	5	21	.244
1949—Brooklyn	National	OF	146	552	100	161	28	7	23	92	.292
1950—Brooklyn	National	OF	152	620	109	199	31	10	31	107	.321
1951—Brooklyn	National	OF	150	606	96	168	26	6	29	101	.277
1952—Brooklyn	National	OF	144	534	80	162	25	7	21	92	.303
1953—Brooklyn	National	OF	153	590	132	198	38	4	42	126	.336
1954—Brooklyn	National	OF	149	584	120	199	39	10	40	130	.341
1955—Brooklyn	National	OF	148	538	126	166	34	6	42	136	.309
1956—Brooklyn	National	OF	151	542	112	158	33	2	43	101	.292
1957—Brooklyn	National	OF	139	508	91	139	25	7	40	92	.274
1958—Los Angeles	National	OF	106	327	45	102	12	3	15	58	.312
1959—Los Angeles	National	OF	126	370	59	114	11	2	23	88	.308
1960—Los Angeles	National	OF	101	235	38	57	13	5	14	36	.243
1961—Los Angeles	National	OF	85	232	35	69	8	3	16	56	.297
Major League Totals			1843	6481	1171	1951	332	79	384	1241	.301

WORLD'S SERIES RECORD

	Club.	League.	Pos.	G.	A.B.	R.	H.	2B.	3B.	HR.	RBI.	B.A.
1949—Brooklyn	National	OF	5	21	2	3	1	0	0	0	.143
1952—Brooklyn	National	OF	7	29	5	10	2	0	4	8	.345
1953—Brooklyn	National	OF	6	25	3	8	3	0	1	5	.320
1955—Brooklyn	National	OF	7	25	5	8	1	0	4	7	.320
1956—Brooklyn	National	OF	7	23	5	7	1	0	1	4	.304
1959—Los Angeles	National	OF	4	10	1	2	0	0	1	2	.200
World's Series Totals			36	133	21	38	8	0	11	26	.286

ALL-STAR GAME RECORD

Year.	League.	Pos.	AB.	R.	H.	2B.	3B.	HR.	RBI.	B.A.
1950—National	PH	1	0	0	0	0	0	0	.000
1951—National	OF	0	0	0	0	0	0	0	.000
1953—National	OF	0	1	0	0	0	0	0	.000
1954—National	OF	4	2	3	1	0	0	0	.750
1955—National	OF	2	0	0	0	0	0	0	.000
1956—National	OF	3	0	0	0	0	0	0	.000
All-Star Game Totals			10	3	3	1	0	0	0	.300

MICKEY CHARLES MANTLE

Born, Oct. 20, 1931, at Spavinaw, Okla.
Height, 5:11 1/2. Weight, 195. Gray eyes and blond hair.
Threw right and batted both right and left-handed

Year.	Club.	League.	Pos.	G.	AB.	R.	H.	2B.	3B.	HR.	RBI.	B.A.
1949—Independence	....	K-O-M	SS	89	323	54	101	15	7	7	63	.313
1950—Joplin	....	W.A.	SS	137	519	141	199	30	12	26	136	.383
1951—New York	....	American	OF	96	341	61	91	11	5	13	65	.267
1951—Kansas City	....	A.A.	OF	40	166	32	60	9	3	11	50	.361
1952—New York	....	American	OF-3B	142	549	94	171	37	7	23	87	.311
1953—New York	....	American	OF-SS	127	461	105	136	24	3	21	92	.295
1954—New York	....	American	OF-IF	146	543	129	163	17	12	27	102	.300
1955—New York	....	American	OF-SS	147	517	121	158	25	11	37	99	.306
1956—New York	....	American	OF	150	533	132	188	22	5	52	130	.353
1957—New York	....	American	OF	144	474	121	173	28	6	34	94	.365
1958—New York	....	American	OF	150	519	127	158	21	1	42	97	.304
1959—New York	....	American	OF	144	541	104	154	23	4	31	75	.285
1960—New York	....	American	OF	153	527	119	145	17	6	40	94	.275
1961—New York	....	American	OF	153	514	131	163	16	6	54	128	.317
Major League Totals	....			1552	5519	1244	1700	241	66	374	1063	.308

WORLD'S SERIES RECORD

Year.	Club.	League.	Pos.	G.	AB.	R.	H.	2B.	3B.	HR.	RBI.	B.A.
1951—New York (a)	....	American	OF	2	5	1	1	0	0	0	0	.200
1952—New York	....	American	OF	7	29	5	10	1	1	2	3	.345
1953—New York	....	American	OF	6	24	3	5	0	0	2	7	.208
1955—New York	....	American	OF	3	10	1	2	0	0	1	1	.200
1956—New York	....	American	OF	7	24	6	6	1	0	3	4	.250
1957—New York	....	American	OF	6	19	3	5	0	0	1	2	.263
1958—New York	....	American	OF	7	24	4	6	0	1	2	3	.250
1960—New York	....	American	OF	7	25	8	10	1	0	3	11	.400
1961—New York	....	American	OF	2	6	0	1	0	0	0	0	.167
World's Series Totals	....			47	166	31	46	3	2	14	31	.277

(a) Injured right knee in fifth inning of second game; did not play for rest of Series.

ALL-STAR GAME RECORD

Year.	League.	Pos.	AB.	R.	H.	2B.	3B.	HR.	RBI.	B.A.
1953—American	....	OF	2	0	0	0	0	0	0	.000
1954—American	....	OF	5	1	2	0	0	0	0	.400
1955—American	....	OF	6	1	2	0	0	1	3	.333
1956—American	....	OF	4	1	1	0	0	1	1	.250
1957—American	....	OF	4	1	1	0	0	0	0	.250
1958—American	....	OF	2	0	1	0	0	0	0	.500
1959—American (both games)	....	OF	3	0	1	0	0	0	0	.333
1960—American (both games)	....	OF	4	0	1	0	0	0	0	.250
1961—American (both games)	....	DF	6	0	0	0	0	0	0	.000
All-Star Totals	....		36	4	9	0	0	2	4	.250

EDWIN LEE MATHEWS, JR.

Born, Oct. 13, 1931, at Texarkana, Tex.
Height, 6:01. Weight, 205. Brown eyes and hair.
Threw right and batted left-handed

Year.	Club.	League.	Pos.	G.	AB.	R.	H.	2B.	3B.	HR.	RBI.	B.A.
1949—H. Point-Th'ville		N.C. St.	3B	63	240	62	87	20	3	17	56	.363
1950—Atlanta		Southern	3B	146	552	103	158	24	9	32	106	.286
1951—Atlanta		Southern	3B	37	128	23	37	5	4	6	29	.289
1951—Milwaukee		A.A.	3B	12	9	2	3	0	0	1	5	.333
1952—Boston		National	3B	145	528	80	128	23	5	25	58	.242
1953—Milwaukee (a)		National	3B	157	579	110	175	31	8	47	135	.302
1954—Milwaukee		National	3B-OF	138	476	96	138	21	4	40	103	.290
1955—Milwaukee		National	3B	141	499	108	144	23	5	41	101	.289
1956—Milwaukee		National	3B	151	552	103	150	21	2	37	95	.272
1957—Milwaukee		National	3B	148	572	109	167	28	9	32	94	.292
1958—Milwaukee		National	3B	149	546	97	137	18	1	31	77	.251
1959—Milwaukee		National	3B	148	594	118	182	16	8	46	114	.306
1960—Milwaukee		National	3B	153	548	108	152	19	7	39	124	.277
1961—Milwaukee		National	3B	152	572	103	175	21	7	32	91	.306
Major League Totals				1482	5466	1032	1548	221	56	370	992	.283

(a) Boston franchise transferred to Milwaukee, March 18, 1953.

WORLD'S SERIES RECORD

Year.	Club.	League.	Pos.	G.	AB.	R.	H.	2B.	3B.	HR.	RBI.	B.A.
1957—Milwaukee		National	3B	7	22	4	5	3	0	1	4	.227
1958—Milwaukee		National	3B	7	25	3	4	2	0	0	3	.160
World's Series Totals				14	47	7	9	5	0	1	7	.191

ALL-STAR GAME RECORD

Year.	League.	Pos.	AB.	R.	H.	2B.	3B.	HR.	RBI.	B.A.
1953—National		3B	3	1	0	0	0	0	0	.000
1955—National		3B	2	0	0	0	0	0	0	.000
1957—National		3B	3	0	0	0	0	0	0	.000
1959—National (both games)		3B-PH	4	• 1	1	0	0	1	1	.250
1960—National (both games)		3B	7	1	1	0	0	1	2	.143
1961—National (both games)		3B	5	1	0	0	0	0	0	.000
All-Star Game Totals			24	4	2	0	0	2	3	.080

RALPH McPHERRAN KINER

Born, Oct. 27, 1922, at Santa Rita, N. M.
Height, 6:02. Weight, 195. Blue eyes and brown hair.
Threw and batted right-handed

Year.	Club.	League.	Pos.	G.	AB.	R.	H.	2B.	3B.	HR.	RBI.	B.A.
1941—Albany		Eastern	OF	141	509	94	142	23	7	11	66	.279
1942—Albany		Eastern	OF	141	483	84	124	27	7	14	75	.257
1943—Toronto		International	OF	43	144	22	34	6	2	2	13	.236
1943-44-45—Pittsburgh		National			(In Military Service)							
1946—Pittsburgh		National	OF	144	502	63	124	17	3	23	81	.247
1947—Pittsburgh		National	OF	152	565	118	177	23	4	51	127	.313
1948—Pittsburgh		National	OF	156	555	104	147	19	5	40	123	.265
1949—Pittsburgh		National	OF	152	549	116	170	19	5	54	127	.310
1950—Pittsburgh		National	OF	150	547	112	149	21	6	47	118	.272
1951—Pittsburgh		National	OF-1B	151	531	124	164	31	6	42	109	.309
1952—Pittsburgh		National	OF	149	516	90	126	17	2	37	87	.244
1953—Pitts.(a) - Chicago		National	OF	158	562	100	157	20	3	35	116	.279
1954—Chicago (b)		National	OF	147	557	88	159	36	5	22	73	.285
1955—Cleveland		American	OF	113	321	56	78	13	0	18	54	.243
National League Totals				1359	4884	915	1373	203	39	351	961	.281
American League Totals				113	321	56	78	13	0	18	54	.243
Major League Totals				1472	5205	971	1451	216	39	369	1015	.279

(a) Traded to Chicago Cubs with Pitcher Howard Pollet, Catcher Joe Garagiola and Outfielder-First Baseman George Metkovich for Pitcher Bob Schultz, Catcher Toby Atwell, First Baseman Preston Ward, Infielder George Freese, Outfielders Bob Addis and Gene Hermanski and estimated $100,000, June 4, 1953.

(b) Traded to Cleveland Indians for Pitcher Sam Jones, Outfielder Gale Wade and estimated $60,000, November 16, 1954.

ALL-STAR GAME RECORD

Year.	League.	Pos.	AB.	R.	H.	2B.	3B.	HR.	RBI.	B.A.
1948—National		OF	1	0	0	0	0	0	0	.000
1949—National		OF	5	1	1	0	0	1	2	.200
1950—National		OF	6	1	2	1	0	1	1	.333
1951—National		OF	2	1	1	0	0	1	1	.500
1953—National		PH	1	0	0	0	0	0	0	.000
All-Star Game Totals			15	3	4	1	0	3	4	.267

JOSEPH PAUL DiMAGGIO

Born, Nov. 25, 1914, at Martinez, Calif.
Height, 6:02. Weight, 195. Brown eyes and black hair.
Threw and batted right-handed

Year.	Club.	League.	Pos.	G.	AB.	R.	H.	2B.	3B.	HR.	RBI.	B.A.
1932—San Francisco		P. C.	SS	3	9	2	2	1	1	0	2*	.222
1933—San Francisco		P. C.	OF	187	762	129	259	45	13	28	169	.340
1934—San Francisco		P. C.	OF	101	375	58	128	18	6	12	69	.341
1935—San Francisco		P. C.	OF	172	679	173	270	58	18	34	154	.398
1936—New York		American	OF	138	637	132	206	44	15	29	125	.323
1937—New York		American	OF	151	621	151	215	35	15	46	167	.346
1938—New York		American	OF	145	599	129	194	32	13	32	140	.324
1939—New York		American	OF	120	462	108	176	32	6	30	126	.381
1940—New York		American	OF	132	508	93	179	28	9	31	133	.352
1941—New York		American	OF	139	541	122	193	43	11	30	125	.357
1942—New York		American	OF	154	610	123	186	29	13	21	114	.305
1943-44-45—New York		American		(In Military Service)								
1946—New York		American	OF	132	503	81	146	20	8	25	95	.290
1947—New York		American	OF	141	534	97	168	31	10	20	97	.315
1948—New York		American	OF	153	594	110	190	26	11	39	155	.320
1949—New York		American	OF	76	272	58	94	14	6	14	67	.346
1950—New York		American	OF-1B	139	525	114	158	33	10	32	122	.301
1951—New York		American	OF	116	415	72	109	22	4	12	71	.263

Major League Totals .... 1736 6821 1390 2214 389 131 361 1537 .325

WORLD'S SERIES RECORD

Year.	Club.	League.	Pos.	G.	AB.	R.	H.	2B.	3B.	HR.	RBI.	B.A.
1936—New York		American	OF	6	26	3	9	3	0	0	3	.346
1937—New York		American	OF	5	22	2	6	0	0	1	4	.273
1938—New York		American	OF	4	15	4	4	0	0	1	2	.267
1939—New York		American	OF	4	16	3	5	0	0	1	3	.313
1941—New York		American	OF	5	19	1	5	0	0	0	1	.263
1942—New York		American	OF	5	21	3	7	0	0	0	3	.333
1947—New York		American	OF	7	26	4	6	0	0	2	5	.231
1949—New York		American	OF	5	18	2	2	0	0	1	2	.111
1950—New York		American	OF	4	13	2	4	1	0	1	2	.308
1951—New York		American	OF	6	23	3	6	2	0	1	5	.261

World's Series Totals .... 51 199 27 54 6 0 8 30 .271

ALL-STAR GAME RECORD

Year.	League.	Pos.	AB.	R.	H.	2B.	3B.	HR.	RBI.	B.A.
1936—American		OF	5	0	0	0	0	0	0	.000
1937—American		OF	4	1	1	0	0	0	0	.250
1938—American		OF	4	1	1	0	0	0	0	.250
1939—American		OF	4	1	1	0	0	1	1	.250
1940—American		OF	4	0	0	0	0	0	0	.000
1941—American		OF	4	3	1	1	0	0	1	.250
1942—American		OF	4	0	2	0	0	0	0	.500
1947—American		OF	3	0	1	0	0	0	0	.333
1948—American		PH	1	0	0	0	0	0	1	.000
1949—American		OF	4	1	2	1	0	0	3	.500
1950—American		OF	3	0	0	0	0	0	0	.000

All-Star Game Totals .... 40 7 9 2 0 1 6 .225

GILBERT RAY HODGES

Born, Apr. 4, 1924, at Princeton, Ind.
Height, 6:02. Weight, 200. Blue eyes and brown hair.
Throw and batted right-handed

Year.	Club.	League.	Pos.	G.	AB.	R.	H.	2B.	3B.	HR.	RBI.	B.A.
1943—Brooklyn		National	3B	1	2	0	0	0	0	0	0	.000
1943-44-45—Brooklyn		National				(In Military Service)						
1946—Newport News		Piedmont	C	129	406	65	113	27	7	8	64	.278
1947—Brooklyn		National	C	28	77	9	12	3	1	1	7	.156
1948—Brooklyn		National	1B-C	134	481	48	120	18	5	11	70	.249
1949—Brooklyn		National	1B	156	596	94	170	23	4	23	115	.285
1950—Brooklyn		National	1B	153	561	98	159	26	2	32	113	.283
1951—Brooklyn		National	1B	158	582	118	156	25	3	40	103	.268
1952—Brooklyn		National	1B	153	508	87	129	27	1	32	102	.254
1953—Brooklyn		National	1B-OF	141	520	101	157	22	7	31	122	.302
1954—Brooklyn		National	1B	154	579	106	176	23	5	42	130	.304
1955—Brooklyn		National	1B-OF	150	546	75	158	24	5	27	102	.289
1956—Brooklyn		National	1B-O-C	153	550	86	146	29	4	32	87	.265
1957—Brooklyn		National	1-3-2B	150	579	94	173	28	7	27	98	.299
1958—Los Angeles		National	1-3-O-C	141	475	68	123	15	1	22	64	.259
1959—Los Angeles		National	1B-3B	124	413	57	114	19	2	25	80	.276
1960—Los Angeles		National	1B-3B	101	197	22	39	8	1	8	30	.198
1961—Los Angeles		National	1B-3B	110	216	25	52	4	0	8	32	.241

Major League Totals .... 2007 6882 1088 1884 294 48 361 1255 .274

WORLD'S SERIES RECORD

Year.	Club.	League.	Pos.	G.	AB.	R.	H.	2B.	3B.	HR.	RBI.	B.A.
1947—Brooklyn		National	PH	1	1	0	0	0	0	0	0	.000
1949—Brooklyn		National	1B	5	17	2	4	0	0	1	4	.235
1952—Brooklyn		National	1B	7	21	1	0	0	0	0	1	.000
1953—Brooklyn		National	1B	6	22	3	8	0	0	1	1	.364
1955—Brooklyn		National	1B	7	24	2	7	0	0	1	5	.292
1956—Brooklyn		National	1B	7	23	5	7	2	0	1	8	.304
1959—Los Angeles		National	1B	6	23	2	9	0	1	1	2	.391

World's Series Totals .... 39 131 15 35 2 1 5 21 .267

ALL-STAR GAME RECORD

Year.	League.	Pos.	AB.	R.	H.	2B.	3B.	HR.	RBI.	B.A.
1949—National		1B	3	1	1	0	0	0	0	.333
1951—National		1B	5	2	2	0	0	1	2	.400
1953—National		1B	1	0	0	0	0	0	0	.000
1954—National		1B	1	0	0	0	0	0	0	.000
1955—National		PH	1	0	1	0	0	0	0	1.000
1957—National		PH	1	0	0	0	0	0	0	.000

All-Star Game Totals .... 12 3 4 0 0 1 2 .333

JOHN ROBERT MIZE

Born, Jan. 7, 1913, at Demorest, Ga.

Height, 6:02. Weight, 215. Gray eyes and brown hair.

Threw right and batted left-handed

Year.	Club.	League.	G.	AB.	R.	H.	2B.	3B.	HR.	RBI.	B.A.
1930—Greensboro		Piedmont	12	31	5	6	3	0	0	2	.194
1931—Greensboro		Piedmont	94	341	69	115	27	1	9	64	.337
1932—Elmira		NYP	106	405	60	132	20	11	8	78	.326
1933—Greensboro		Piedmont	98	378	108	136	29	10	22	104	.369
1933—Rochester		International	42	159	27	56	11	3	8	32	.352
1934—Rochester		International	90	313	49	106	16	1	17	66	.339
1935—Rochester		International	65	252	37	80	11	1	12	44	.317
1936—St. Louis		National	126	414	76	136	30	8	19	93	.329
1937—St. Louis		National	145	560	103	204	40	7	25	113	.364
1938—St. Louis		National	149	531	85	179	34	16	27	102	.337
1939—St. Louis		National	153	564	104	197	44	14	28	108	.349
1940—St. Louis		National	155	579	111	182	31	13	43	137	.314
1941—St. Louis (a)		National	126	473	67	150	39	8	16	100	.317
1942—New York		National	142	541	97	165	25	7	26	110	.305
1943-44-45—New York		National			(In Military Service)						
1946—New York		National	101	377	70	127	18	3	22	70	.337
1947—New York		National	154	586	137	177	26	2	51	138	.302
1948—New York		National	152	560	110	162	26	4	40	125	.289
1949—New York (b)		National	106	388	59	102	15	0	18	62	.263
1949—New York		American	13	23	4	6	1	0	1	2	.261
1950—Kansas City		A. A.	26	94	18	28	4	0	5	18	.298
1950—New York		American	90	274	43	76	12	0	25	72	.277
1951—New York		American	113	332	37	86	14	1	10	49	.259
1952—New York		American	78	137	9	36	9	0	4	29	.263
1953—New York		American	81	104	6	26	3	0	4	27	.250

Major League Totals ....1884 6443 1118 2011 367 83 359 1337 .312

(a) Traded to New York Giants for Catcher James K. O'Dea, Pitcher Bill Lohrman, First Baseman Johnny McCarthy (assigned to Columbus A. A. club) and $50,000, December 11, 1941. However, Commissioner Landis later upheld Indianapolis' claim to McCarthy as per a prior agreement.

(b) Sold to New York Yankees for $40,000, August 22, 1949.

WORLD'S SERIES RECORD

Year.	Club.	League.	G.	AB.	R.	H.	2B.	3B.	HR.	RBI.	B.A.
1949—New York		American	2	2	0	2	0	0	0	2	1.000
1950—New York		American	4	15	0	2	0	0	0	0	.333
1951—New York		American	4	7	2	2	1	0	0	1	.286
1952—New York		American	5	15	3	6	1	0	3	6	.400
1953—New York		American	3	3	0	0	0	0	0	0	.000

World's Series Totals .... 16 42 5 12 2 0 3 9 .286

LAWRENCE PETER BERRA

Born, May 12, 1925, at St. Louis, Mo.
Height, 5:08. Weight, 191. Brown eyes and black hair.
Threw right and batted left-handed

Year.	Club.	League.	Pos.	G.	AB.	R.	H.	2B.	3B.	HR.	RBI.	B.A.
1943—Norfolk		Piedmont	C	111	376	52	95	17	8	7	56	.253
1944-55—Kansas City		A. A.			(In Military Service)							
1946—Newark		International	C-OF	77	277	41	87	14	1	15	59	.314
1946—New York		American	C	7	22	3	8	1	0	2	4	.364
1947—New York		American	C-OF	83	293	41	82	15	3	11	54	.280
1948—New York		American	C-OF	125	469	70	143	24	10	14	98	.305
1949—New York		American	C	116	415	59	115	20	2	20	91	.277
1950—New York		American	C	151	597	116	192	30	6	28	124	.322
1951—New York		American	C	141	547	92	161	19	4	27	88	.294
1952—New York		American	C	142	534	97	146	17	1	30	98	.273
1953—New York		American	C	137	503	80	149	23	5	27	108	.296
1954—New York		American	C-3B	151	584	88	179	28	6	22	125	.307
1955—New York		American	C	147	541	84	147	20	3	27	108	.272
1956—New York		American	C-OF	140	521	93	155	29	2	30	105	.298
1957—New York		American	C-OF	134	482	74	121	14	2	24	82	.251
1958—New York		American	C-OF-1B	122	433	60	115	17	3	22	90	.266
1959—New York		American	C-OF	131	472	64	134	25	1	19	69	.284
1960—New York		American	C-OF	120	359	46	99	14	1	15	62	.276
1961—New York		American	C-OF	119	395	62	107	12	0	22	61	.271
Major League Totals				1966	7167	1129	2053	308	49	340	1367	.286

WORLD'S SERIES RECORD

Year.	Club.	League.	Pos.	G.	AB.	R.	H.	2B.	3B.	HR.	RBI.	B.A.
1947—New York		American	C-OF	6	19	2	3	0	0	1	2	.158
1949—New York		American	C	4	16	2	1	0	0	0	1	.063
1950—New York		American	C	4	15	2	3	0	0	1	2	.200
1951—New York		American	C	6	23	4	6	1	0	0	0	.261
1952—New York		American	C	7	28	2	6	1	0	2	3	.214
1953—New York		American	C	6	21	3	9	1	0	1	4	.429
1955—New York		American	C	7	24	5	10	1	0	1	2	.417
1956—New York		American	C	7	25	5	9	2	0	3	10	.360
1957—New York		American	C	7	25	5	8	1	0	0	2	.320
1958—New York		American	C	7	27	3	6	3	0	0	2	.222
1960—New York		American	C-OF-PH	7	22	6	7	0	0	1	8	.318
1961—New York		American	OF	4	11	2	3	0	0	1	3	.273
World's Series Totals				72	254	41	71	10	0	12	39	.280

ALL-STAR GAME RECORD

Year.	League.	Pos.	AB.	R.	H.	2B.	3B.	HR.	RBI.	B.A.
1949—American		C	3	0	0	0	0	0	0	.000
1950—American		C	2	0	0	0	0	0	0	.000
1951—American		C	4	1	1	0	0	0	0	.250
1952—American		C	2	0	0	0	0	0	0	.000
1953—American		C	4	0	0	0	0	0	0	.000
1954—American		C	4	2	2	0	0	0	0	.500
1955—American		C	6	1	1	0	0	0	0	.167
1956—American		C	2	0	2	0	0	0	0	1.000
1957—American		C	3	0	1	0	0	0	1	.333
1958—American		C	2	0	0	0	0	0	0	.000
1961—American (first game only)		C	1	0	0	0	0	0	0	.000
All-Star Game Totals			33	4	7	0	0	0	1	.201

HENRY BENJAMIN GREENBERG

Born, Jan. 1, 1911, at New York, N. Y.
Height, 6:04. Weight, 215. Brown eyes and hair.
Throw and batted right-handed

Year. Club. League.	G.	AB.	R.	H.	2B.	3B.	HR.	RBI.	B.A.
1930—Hartford ....Eastern	17	56	10	12	1	3	2	6	.214
1930—Raleigh ....Piedmont	122	452	88	142	26	14	19	93	.314
1930—Detroit ....American	1	1	0	0	0	0	0	0	.000
1931—Evansville............I. I. I.	126	487	88	155	41	10	15	85	.318
1931—Beaumont...............Texas	3	2	0	0	0	0	0	0	.000
1932—Beaumont.............Texas	154	600	123	174	31	11	39	131	.290
1933—Detroit ....American	117	449	59	135	33	3	12	87	.301
1934—Detroit ....American	153	593	118	201	63	7	26	139	.339
1935—Detroit ....American	152	619	121	203	46	16	36	170	.328
1936—Detroit ....American	12	46	10	16	6	2	1	16	.348
1937—Detroit ....American	154	594	137	200	49	14	40	183	.337
1938—Detroit ....American	155	556	144	175	23	4	58	146	.315
1939—Detroit ....American	138	500	112	156	42	7	33	112	.312
1940—Detroit ....American	148	573	129	195	50	8	41	150	.340
1941—Detroit ....American	19	67	12	18	5	1	2	12	.269
1942-43-44—Detroit.........American	(In Military Service)								
1945—Detroit ....American	78	270	47	84	20	2	13	60	.311
1946—Detroit (a) ....American	142	523	91	145	29	5	44	127	.277
1947—Pittsburgh (b) ....National	125	402	71	100	13	2	25	74	.249
Major League Totals	1394	5193	1051	1628	379	71	331	1276	.313

(a) Sold to Pittsburgh Pirates for undisclosed sum, January 18, 1947.

(b) Released unconditionally by Pittsburgh Pirates, September 29, 1947, and joined Cleveland Indians' front office, March 27, 1948.

WORLD'S SERIES RECORD

Year. Club. League.	G.	AB.	R.	H.	2B.	3B.	HR.	RBI.	B.A.
1934—Detroit ....American	7	28	4	9	2	1	1	7	.321
1935—Detroit ....American	2	6	1	1	0	0	1	2	.167
1940—Detroit ....American	7	28	5	10	2	1	1	6	.357
1945—Detroit ....American	7	23	7	7	3	0	2	7	.304
World's Series Totals	23	85	17	27	7	2	5	22	.318

WILLIE HOWARD MAYS, JR.

Born, May 6, 1931, at Fairfield, Ala.

Height, 5:10 1/2. Weight, 180. Brown eyes and black hair.

Threw and batted right-handed

Year.	Club.	League.	Pos.	G.	AB.	R.	H.	2B.	3B.	HR.	RBI.	B.A.
1950—Trenton		Int.-St.	OF	81	306	50	108	20	8	4	55	.353
1951—Minneapolis		A. A.	OF	35	149	38	71	18	3	8	30	.477
1951—New York		National	OF	121	464	59	127	22	5	20	68	.274
1952—New York (a)		National	OF	34	127	17	30	2	4	4	23	.236
1953—New York		National			(In Military Service)							
1954—New York		National	OF	151	565	119	195	33	13	41	110	.345
1955—New York		National	OF	152	580	123	185	18	13	51	127	.319
1956—New York		National	OF	152	578	101	171	27	8	36	84	.296
1957—New York		National	OF	152	585	112	195	26	20	35	97	.333
1958—San Francisco		National	OF	152	600	121	208	33	11	29	96	.347
1959—San Francisco		National	OF	151	575	125	180	43	5	34	104	.313
1960—San Francisco		National	OF	153	595	107	190	29	12	29	103	.319
1961—San Francisco		National	OF	154	572	129	176	32	3	40	123	.308
Major League Totals				1372	5241	1013	1657	265	94	319	935	.316

(a) In Military Service most of season.

WORLD'S SERIES RECORD

Year.	Club.	League.	Pos.	G.	AB.	R.	H.	2B.	3B.	HR.	RBI.	B.A.
1951—New York		National	OF	6	22	1	4	0	0	0	1	.182
1954—New York		National	OF	4	14	4	4	1	0	0	3	.286
World's Series Totals				10	36	5	8	1	0	0	4	.222

ALL-STAR GAME RECORD

Year.	League.	Pos.	AB.	R.	H.	2B.	3B.	HR.	RBI.	B.A.
1954—National		OF	2	1	1	0	0	0	0	.500
1955—National		OF	3	2	2	0	0	0	0	.667
1956—National		OF	3	2	1	0	0	1	2	.333
1957—National		OF	4	2	2	0	1	0	1	.500
1958—National		OF	4	2	1	0	0	0	0	.250
1959—National (both games)		OF	8	0	1	0	1	0	1	.125
1960—National (both games)		OF	8	2	6	1	1	1	1	.750
1961—National (both games)		OF	8	2	3	1	0	0	1	.375
All-Star Game Totals			41	12	17	2	3	2	6	.401

ALOYSIUS HARRY SIMMONS

Born, May 22, 1903, at Milwaukee, Wis.
Height, 6:00. Weight, 210. Gray eyes and brown hair.
Threw and batted right-handed

Year.	Club.	League.	G.	AB.	R.	H.	2B.	3B.	HR.	RBI.	B.A.
1922—Aberdeen		Dakota	99	395	91	144	26	16	10	...	.365
1922—Milwaukee		A. A.	19	50	9	11	2	1	1	7	.220
1923—Shreveport		Texas	144	525	96	189	36	10	12	99	.360
1923—Milwaukee		A. A.	24	98	20	39	2	3	0	16	.398
1924—Philadelphia		American	152	594	69	183	31	9	8	102	.308
1925—Philadelphia		American	153	658	122	253	43	12	24	129	.384
1926—Philadelphia		American	147	581	90	199	53	10	19	109	.343
1927—Philadelphia		American	106	406	86	159	36	11	15	108	.392
1928—Philadelphia		American	119	464	78	163	33	9	15	107	.351
1929—Philadelphia		American	143	581	114	212	41	9	34	157	.365
1930—Philadelphia		American	138	554	152	211	41	16	36	165	.381
1931—Philadelphia		American	128	513	105	200	37	13	22	128	.390
1932—Philadelphia (a)		American	154	670	144	216	28	9	35	151	.322
1933—Chicago		American	146	605	85	200	29	10	14	119	.331
1934—Chicago		American	138	558	102	192	36	7	18	104	.344
1935—Chicago (b)		American	128	525	68	140	22	7	16	79	.267
1936—Detroit		American	143	568	96	186	38	6	13	112	.327
1937—Washington (c)		American	103	419	60	117	21	10	8	84	.279
1938—Washington (d)		American	125	470	79	142	23	6	21	95	.302
1939—Boston (e)											
	Cincinnati (f)	National	102	351	39	96	17	7	7	44	.274
1940—Philadelphia		American	37	81	7	25	4	0	1	19	.309
1941—Philadelphia		American	9	24	1	3	1	0	0	1	.125
1942—Philadelphia (g)		American				(Served as coach)					
1943—Boston (h)		American	40	133	9	27	5	0	1	12	.203
1944—Philadelphia		American	4	6	1	3	0	0	0	2	.500

Major League Totals .... 2215 8761 1507 2927 539 149 307 1827 .334

(a) Sold with Third Baseman Jimmie Dykes and Outfielder George Haas for $150,000 to Chicago White Sox, September 28, 1935.

(b) Sold to Detroit Tigers for $75,000, December 10, 1935.

(c) Purchased by Washington Senators for $15,000, April 4, 1937.

(d) Sold to Boston Braves, December 20, 1938.

(e) Sold to Cincinnati Reds, August 31, 1939.

(f) Released by Cincinnati Reds' after season closed and signed by Philadelphia Athletics as free agent, December 11, 1939.

(g) Released following 1942 season and signed by Boston Red Sox as active player, February 2, 1943.

(h) Released by Boston Red Sox, October 15, 1943, and signed as player-coach by Philadelphia Athletics, December, 1943.

WORLD'S SERIES RECORD

Year.	Club.	League.	G.	AB.	R.	H.	2B.	3B.	HR.	RBI.	B.A.
1929—Philadelphia		American	5	20	6	6	1	0	2	5	.300
1930—Philadelphia		American	6	22	4	8	2	0	2	4	.364
1931—Philadelphia		American	7	27	4	9	2	0	2	8	.333
1939—Cincinnati		National	1	4	1	1	1	0	0	0	.250

World's Series Totals .... 19 73 15 24 6 0 6 17 .329

ALL-STAR GAME RECORD

Year.	League.		AB.	R.	H.	2B.	3B.	HR.	RBI.	B.A.
1933—American			4	0	1	0	0	0	0	.250
1934—American			5	3	3	2	0	0	1	.600
1935—American			4	0	2	1	0	0	0	.500

All-Star Game Totals .... 13 3 6 3 0 0 1 .462

ROGERS HORNSBY

Born, April 27, 1896, at Winters, Tex.
Height, 5:11 1/2. Weight, 200. Hazel eyes and brown hair.
Threw and batted right-handed

Year. Club. League.	Pos.	G.	AB.	R.	H.	2B.	3B.	HR.	RBI.	B.A.
1914—Hugo-Denison ....Tex.-Okla.	SS	113	393	47	91	12	3	3	...	.232
1915—Denison ....W. A.	SS	119	429	75	119	26	2	4	...	.277
1915—St. Louis ....National	SS	18	57	5	14	2	0	0	4	.246
1916—St. Louis ....National	INF	139	495	63	155	17	15	6	60	.313
1917—St. Louis ....National	SS·	145	523	86	171	24	17	8	70	.327
1918—St. Louis ....National	SS	115	416	51	117	19	11	5	59	.281
1919—St. Louis ....National	INF	138	512	68	163	15	9	8	68	.318
1920—St. Louis ....National	2B	149	589	96	218	44	20	9	94	.370
1921—St. Louis ....National	INF-OF	154	592	131	235	44	18	21	126	.397
1922—St. Louis ....National	2B	154	623	141	250	46	14	42	152	.401
1923—St. Louis ....National	2B	107	424	89	163	32	10	17	83	.384
1924—St. Louis ....National	2B	143	536	121	227	43	14	25	94	.424
1925—St. Louis ....National	2B	138	504	133	203	41	10	39	143	.403
1926—St. Louis (a) ....National	2B	134	527	96	167	34	5	11	93	.317
1927—New York (b).........National	2B	155	568	133	205	32	9	26	125	.361
1928—Boston (c).. ....National	2B	140	486	99	188	42	7	21	94	.387
1929—Chicago ....National	2B	156	602	156	229	47	7	40	149	.380
1930—Chicago ....National	2B	42	104	15	32	5	1	2	18	.308
1931—Chicago ....National	2B-3B	100	357	64	118	37	1	16	90	.331
1932—Chicago (d) ....National	OF-3B	19	58	10	13	2	0	1	7	.224
1933—St. Louis (e) ....National	2B	46	83	9	27	6	0	2	21	.325
1933—St. Louis ....American	PH	11	9	2	3	1	0	1	2	.333
1934—St. Louis ....American	3B-OF	24	23	2	7	2	0	1	11	.304
1935—St. Louis ....American	INF	10	24	1	5	3	0	0	3	.208
1936—St. Louis ....American	1B	2	5	1	2	0	0	0	2	.400
1937—St. Louis (f) ....American	2B	20	56	7	18	3	0	1	11	.321
1938—Baltimore............International	2B-1B-OF	16	27	2	2	0	0	0	0	.074
1938—Chattanooga ....Southern	2B	3	3	1	2	0	0	1	2	.667
1939—Baltimore ....International				(Did not play)						
1940—Oklahoma City ....Texas	PH	1	1	0	1	0	0	0	0	1.000
1942—Fort Worth ....Texas	2B	1	4	0	1	0	0	0	2	.250
National League Totals		2192	8056	1566	2895	532	168	299	1550	.359
American League Totals		67	117	13	35	9	0	3	29	.299
Major League Totals		2259	8173	1579	2930	541	168	302	1579	.358

(a) Traded to New York Giants for Second Baseman Frank Frisch and Pitcher Jimmy Ring.

(b) Traded to Boston Braves for Catcher Francis (Shanty) Hogan and Outfielder Jimmy Welsh, January 10, 1928.

(c) Traded to Chicago Cubs for Pitchers Percy Jones, Harry Seibold and Bruce Cunningham, Catcher Louis (Doc) Leggett, Second Baseman Fred Maguire and $200,000, November 7, 1928.

(d) Unconditionally released by Chicago Cubs, August 2, 1932; signed with St. Louis Cardinals, October 24, 1932.

(e) Unconditionally released by St. Louis Cardinals, July 25, 1933 and signed as manager of St. Louis Browns following day.

(f) Unconditionally released as manager and player by St. Louis Browns, July 21, 1937.

WORLD'S SERIES RECORD

Year. Club. League.	Pos.	G.	AB.	R.	H.	2B.	3B.	HR.	RBI.	B.A.
1926—St. Louis ....National	2B	7	28	2	7	1	0	0	4	.250
1929—Chicago ....National	2B	5	21	4	5	1	1	0	1	.238
World's Series Totals		12	49	6	12	2	1	0	5	.245

CHARLES HERBERT KLEIN

Born, Oct. 7, 1905, at Indianapolis, Ind.
Height, 6:00. Weight, 195. Brown eyes and hair.
Threw right and batted left-handed

Year.	Club.	League.	Pos.	G.	AB.	R.	H.	2B.	3B.	HR.	RBI.	B.A.
1927	Evansville	I. I. I.	OF-1B	14	49	10	16	2	2	2	...	.327
1928	Fort Wayne	Cent.	OF	88	359	85	119	29	4	26	...	.331
1928	Philadelphia	National	OF	64	253	41	91	14	4	11	34	.360
1929	Philadelphia	National	OF	149	616	126	219	45	6	43	145	.356
1930	Philadelphia	National	OF	156	648	158	250	59	8	40	170	.386
1931	Philadelphia	National	OF	148	594	121	200	34	10	31	121	.337
1932	Philadelphia	National	OF	154	650	152	226	50	15	38	137	.348
1933	Philadelphia (a)	National	OF	152	606	101	223	44	7	28	120	.368
1934	Chicago	National	OF	115	435	78	131	27	2	20	80	.301
1935	Chicago	National	OF	119	434	71	127	14	4	21	73	.293
1936	Chicago (b)-Phila.	National	OF	146	601	102	184	35	7	25	104	.306
1937	Philadelphia	National	OF	115	406	74	132	20	2	15	57	.325
1938	Philadelphia	National	OF	129	458	53	113	22	2	8	61	.247
1939	Phila.(c)-Pitts.(d)	National	OF	110	317	45	90	18	5	12	56	.284
1940	Philadelphia	National	OF	116	354	49	77	16	2	7	37	.218
1941	Philadelphia	National	OF-PH	50	73	6	9	0	0	1	3	.123
1942	Philadelphia	National	PH	14	14	0	1	0	0	0	0	.071
1943	Philadelphia	National	PH-OF	12	20	0	2	0	0	0	3	.100
1944	Philadelphia	National	PH-OF	4	7	1	1	0	0	0	0	.143

Major League Totals ....1753 6486 1178 2076 398 74 300 1201 .320

(a) Traded to Chicago Cubs for Pitcher Ted Kleinhans, Infielder Mark Koenig and Outfielder Harvey Hendrick and $65,000, November 21, 1933.

(b) Traded with Pitcher Fabian Kowalik and $50,000 to Philadelphia Phillies for Outfielder Ethan Allen and Pitcher Curtis Davis, May 21, 1936.

(c) Released by Philadelphia Phillies and signed by Pittsburgh, June 7, 1939.

(d) Released by Pittsburgh and signed by Philadelphia Phillies, March 26, 1940.

WORLD'S SERIES RECORD

Year.	Club.	League.	Pos.	G.	AB.	R.	H.	2B.	3B.	HR.	RBI.	B.A.
1935	Chicago	National	OF	5	12	2	4	0	0	1	2	.333

ALL-STAR GAME RECORD

Year.	League.	Pos.	AB.	R.	H.	2B.	3B.	HR.	RBI.	B.A.
1933	National	OF	4	0	1	0	0	0	0	.250
1934	National	OF	3	0	1	0	0	0	1	.333

All-Star Game Totals .... 7 0 2 0 0 0 1 .286

Coach, Philadelphia Phillies, 1942 through 1945.

ROGER EUGENE MARIS

Born, Sept. 10, 1934, at Hibbing, Minn.
Height, 6:00. Weight, 197. Green eyes and brown hair.
Threw right and batted left-handed

Year. Club.	League.	Pos.	G.	AB.	R.	H.	2B.	3B.	HR.	RBI.	B.A.
1953—Fargo-M'rhead	Northern	OF	114	418	74	136	18	13	9	80	.325
1954—Keokuk	I. I. I.	OF	134	502	105	158	26	6	32	111	.315
1955—Tulsa...............	Texas	OF	25	90	9	21	1	0	1	9	.233
1955—Reading	Eastern	OF	113	374	74	108	15	3	19	78	.289
1956—Indianapolis	A. A.	OF	131	433	77	127	20	8	17	75	.293
1957—Cleveland...........	American	OF	116	358	61	84	9	5	14	51	.235
1958—Cleveland (a)- K. C. ..	American	OF	150	583	87	140	19	4	28	80	.240
1959—Kansas City (b)	American	OF	122	433	69	118	21	7	16	72	.273
1960—New York	American	OF	136	499	98	141	18	7	39	112	.283
1961—New York	American	OF	161	590	132	159	16	4	61	142	.269
Major League Totals			685	2463	447	642	83	27	158	457	.260

(a) Traded to Kansas City Athetics with Pitcher Dick Tomanek and Infielder Preston Ward for Infielder Vic Power and Infielder-Outfielder Woodie Held, June 15, 1958.

(b) Traded to New York Yankees with First Baseman Kent Hadley and Shortstop Joe DeMaestri for Pitcher Don Larsen, First Baseman Marv Throneberry and Outfielders Hank Bauer and Norm Siebern, December 11, 1959.

WORLD'S SERIES RECORD

Year. Club.	League.	Pos.	G.	AB.	R.	H.	2B.	3B.	HR.	RBI.	B.A.
1960—New York	American	OF	7	30	6	8	1	0	2	2	.267
1961—New York	American	OF	5	19	4	2	1	0	1	2	.105
World's Series Totals			12	49	10	10	2	0	3	4	.204

ALL-STAR GAME RECORD

Year. League.		Pos.	AB.	R.	H.	2B.	3B.	HR.	RBI.	B.A.
1959—American (second game)		OF	2	0	0	0	0	0	0	.000
1960—American (both games)..........................		OF	6	0	0	0	0	0	0	.000
1961—American (both games)..........................		OF	5	0	1	0	0	0	0	.200
All-Star Game Totals			13	0	1	0	0	0	0	.070

INDEX

Index